COLOR THEORY

ART AND ARCHITECTURE INFORMATION GUIDE SERIES

Series Editor: Sydney Starr Keaveney,
Associate Professor, Pratt Institute Library

Also in the Art and Architecture Series:

AMERICAN PAINTING—*Edited by Sydney Starr Keaveney*

AMERICAN ARCHITECTURE FROM THE CIVIL WAR TO WORLD WAR I—*Edited by Lawrence Wodehouse**

AMERICAN ARCHITECTURE FROM WORLD WAR I TO THE PRESENT—*Edited by Lawrence Wodehouse**

ART THERAPY—*Edited by Josef E. Garai***

ART EDUCATION—*Edited by Clarence Bunch***

AMERICAN SCULPTURE—*Edited by Janis Ekdahl***

CERAMICS—*Edited by James Edward Campbell***

MODERN EUROPEAN PAINTING—*Edited by Ann-Marie Bergholtz***

INDUSTRIAL DESIGN—*Edited by J. Roger Guilfoyle***

PHOTOGRAPHY—*Edited by Diana Edkins***

PRINTS AND PRINTING—*Edited by Jeffrey Wortman***

*in press
** in preparation

The above series is part of the
GALE INFORMATION GUIDE LIBRARY

The Library consists of a number of separate series of guides covering major areas in the social sciences, humanities, and current affairs.

General Editor: Paul Wasserman, Professor and former Dean, School of Library and Information Services, University of Maryland

COLOR THEORY

A GUIDE TO INFORMATION SOURCES

Volume 2 in the Art and Architecture
Information Guide Series

Mary Buckley

Professor of Art, Color, and Design, Pratt Institute

David Baum

Assistant editor

Gale Research Company
Book Tower, Detroit, Michigan 48226

Library of Congress
Cataloging in Publication Data

Buckley, Mary L
  Color theory.

  (Art and architecture information guide series ;
v. 2) (Gale information guide library)
  1. Color--Bibliography. 2. Color-sense--
Bibliography. 3. Color--Psychology--Bibliography.
I. Baum, David W. II. Title.
Z7144.C7B8   016.701'8   73-17517

VITAE

Mary Buckley, IDSA, is a professor of art, color, and design, The Art School, Pratt Institute, and the director of the Margaret Gate Institute, Huntington, New York. She is an artist and educator who has had painting exhibitions in numerous galleries, including the Waverly, Marino, and Caravan Galleries in New York City. Her murals and sculptures are represented in many public and private buildings; they include sculptures for the New York State Legislature Building in Albany and murals in the Seagram Building, New York City. She received a grant from the New York State Council on the Arts to act as artist and concept director for the Bronx State Children's Psychiatric Hospital.

Ms. Buckley received her education at Keuka College, Yale University Art School, the Brooklyn Museum Art School, and The New School. She has studied with Victor Candell and Hans Hofmann. She is married to Joseph M. Parriott.

David William Baum is currently a candidate for a Master of Industrial Design degree at Pratt Institute. He received his B.A. from the University of Nebraska. He has held administrative positions at Pratt Institute where he was responsible for organizing the new office of Programming and Counseling for the School of Art and Design.

CONTENTS

Contents

INTRODUCTION

Color is light as light is color. The reality of this thought may be grasped when light is considered as a stimulus and color as the result. Color as an effect of light has a profound psychophysiological affect upon us. Color heightens our visual awareness, calling our attention to new visual phenomena in varying situations and often creating a sense of wonderment. Color may become an activating stimulus as we perceive the world during moments of passivity, as when a brightly colored bird enters our peripheral vision. We may actively analyze color relationships and interacting color phenomena through the cone of vision, as in discovering the nauances of any flower, or two colors with varying or even similar attributes perceived side by side. The artist makes constant visual color decisions and poses color questions as he observes nature or studies his own work. He usually learns about color by his involvement with it. However, he may wish to learn more about the subject in other environments. And this is the purpose of this bibliography.

Putting together a color bibliography was from the beginning a complex challenge, as color is inclined to be claimed as the property of all: for everyone feels he sees, uses, and knows color. The discipline and knowledge necessary to consciously perceive color ranges into such spheres of knowledge as color studies in science, in psychology, in chemistry, in painting, in literature, and in the artist's writings and observations.

This bibliography is for the artist interested in the pursuit of the mysteries of color and is not intended to supply information about books that will tell anyone "how to" apply color in any of the visual arts. Rather, I have included those sources that have influenced the concepts, theories, and particularly the paintings of practicing artists. Books have been included that were source material for artists who wrote about color for educational reasons as well as those that stimulated lyrical ideas.

I have been delighted to include my favorite books that refer directly to nature for visual (stimulus) learning. Winston Churchill's book on painting was included because of his freshness and directness of perception as well as his deep reverence and love of color. His views are not unique but reinforcing.

It is in some ways unfortunate that books about painters who have made unique contributions to the history and development of color awareness, color concepts, and color ideology are rarely dominant about color, but the books selected for this bibliography were chosen because they contain enough references to color to make them valuable documents. However, W. I. Homer's book about Seurat is a splendid exception. A favorite of mine, it is lucid and able to encompass diverse fields of knowledge that influenced Seurat's theories and work. I have also tried to include books about painters who reflect the particular goals of light and color of their time, such as the excellent books on Vermeer and Rembrandt.

Few artists write about their perception of light and color in nature, or make efforts to develop concepts of the psychological effects of color. Goethe, the naturalist, philosopher and dramatist, does, and several translations of his work are included. Artists are more inclined to write about the way to solve some of their problems through the use of pigment (paint) relying upon the physical object - the work of art - to express their insights and feelings. Of course, Paul Klee, Wassily Kandinsky, the Delauneys as well as Leonardo were beautiful exceptions.

The selection of standard science references was based upon their value as a direct influence in the development of an artist's technique, as well as potential sources for new interpretations in color theory.

I have also included books on the psychology of perception, a new and fascinating field for many artists. James J. Gibson is one of the most articulate writers, and as a painter and educator I felt his work to be of the utmost importance. Rudolf Arnheim makes an intelligent and thoughtful argument which links the psychology of perception, from the area of the social sciences, to ideas on visual relationship directly related to the color needs of the artist.

Mr. David W. Baum, a designer who worked with me on this bibliography, and I were pleased to discover the excellent color resources available in the libraries of the New York City area, particularly the Pratt Institute Library, the Yale University Library, the Donnell Library, and the Central Research Collection of the New York Public Library.

An asterisk next to the title of a book, indicates a work which we feel would make an excellent beginning for an individual or librarian interested in creating a relevant section on color in their libraries.

Mary L. Buckley

Chapter 1

COLOR: ADAPTATION

Chapter 1

COLOR: ADAPTATION

Cott, Hugh B. ADAPTIVE COLORATION IN ANIMALS. Introduction by
Julian S. Huxley. New York: Oxford University Press, 1940. xxxii, 508 pp.
Black and white illus., 48 monotone plates, photos. Bibliography.

> Dr. Cott applied optical and psychological principles to analyze the
> visual in "all aesthetic animals (those animals capable of color adap-
> tation)," he carried his findings to fascinating degrees of refinement.
> The subjects of color adaptation and mimetic adaptations are beautifully
> handled.

Simon, Hilda. THE SPLENDOR OF IRIDESCENCE; STRUCTURAL COLORS IN
THE ANIMAL WORLD. New York: Dodd, Mead & Co., (c. 1971). 267 pp.
Illus. by author (mostly color). Bibliography.

> An examination and analysis of structural colors, or the chemistry of
> animal pigmentation and the effects in light, particularly the effects
> of iridescent and metallic hues. Interesting.

Chapter 2

COLOR: AESTHETICS

Chapter 2

COLOR: AESTHETICS

Ashmore, Jerome. SANTAYANA, ART, AND AESTHETICS. Cleveland: The Press of Western Reserve University, 1966. xii, 139 pp.

Color is extremely important to Santayana's consideration of the aesthetic experience. He weighs the subjective and objective qualities of color as part of an object contrasted to a part of subjective experience. To the extent that his aesthetic is moral, he includes the concept of a moral "glow" in his writings.

Berenson, Bernhard. AESTHETICS AND HISTORY IN THE VISUAL ARTS. New York: Pantheon Books, Inc., (c. 1948). 260 pp. Black and white illus.

Berenson's civilized sensibility breeds points of view and ideas that are always refreshing and become more so as time and thought seem less and less valued. He felt that color was indulged in when brain was subordinated to muscle, and also believed color was the servant of shape and pattern as a means to rapid visual interpretation.

Blanshard, Frances Bradshaw. RETREAT FROM LIKENESS IN THE THEORY OF PAINTING. 2nd ed., rev., enl. New York: Columbia University Press, (c. 1945, 1949). 178 pp. Black and white illus.

Frances Blanshard develops a theory in which color is one of the principal factors in the retreat from likeness in painting, beginning with the ideas of Aristotle and Plato, to the paintings of Zeuxis and Parrhasios to the Van Eycks, Leonardo, the Flemish, the Renaissance, Impressionism to Abstract Art. A thoughtful and fascinating study, well researched and documented.

*Dewey, John. ART AS EXPERIENCE. New York: Capricorn Books, (c. 1934, 1958). vii, 355 pp. Preface. Paperbound.

John Dewey includes color interaction of colors as a quality of the senses that has an aesthetic basis. He argues for training the eye to be able to see color abstractly, but suggests that we transfer the values relating color to the things color qualifies. His color theory rests upon Cezanne's concept of the complementary relationship of color and form.

Gilbert, Katharine Everett, and Kuhn, Helmut. A HISTORY OF ESTHETICS. New York: The Macmillan Company, (c. 1939). xx, 582 pp.

> The authors' efforts to establish aesthetic terms or broad definitions include the following theories of color: Plato's theory of color – as an attribute of intellectual form; St. Augustine's – color as an agreeable attribute of beauty; Pliny's – progress from monochrome to polychrome color; and Corneille's – the concept of "social" color. Tantalizing enought to send readers to original sources.

Gilson, Etienne. PAINTING AND REALITY. The A. W. Mellon Lectures in the Fine Arts, 1955, National Gallery of Art, Washington, Bollingen Series, vol. 35, no. 4. New York: Pantheon Books, Inc., (c. 1957). xxiv, 367 pp. Black and white illus. Bibliography. Paperbound.

> A philosopher asking what a philosopher may learn from painting is the stated intention of the book. The logical questioning of the relationship between the science of color and the art of color, between light in nature and color pigments on a canvas, ultimately leads Gilson to the perception of color in sounds (as in music). Although the book is primarily about painting, the author's interest in color is meaningful to the study of color theory.

Goethe, Johann Wolfgang von. See: COLOR: THEORIES. Goethe, Johann Wolfgang von. THEORY OF COLOURS; Matthaei, Rupprecht, ed. GOETHE'S COLOR THEORY; Schindler, Maria, and Merry, Eleanor C. PURE COLOR: TOWARDS A NEW CULTURE.

Harrison, Jane Ellen. ANCIENT ART AND RITUAL. New York: Henry Holt and Co.; London: William and Norgate, (c. 1913). vi, 256 pp. Bibliography.

> Jane Harrison examines color used symbolically in her fascinating analysis of the interaction between art and ritual in ancient times.

Ortega y Gasset, Jose. THE DEHUMANIZATION OF ART, AND OTHER ESSAYS ON ART, CULTURE, AND LITERATURE. Translated by Helene Weyl, et al. Princeton: Princeton University Press, (c. 1948, 1968). 204 pp. Paperbound.

> Ortega y Gasset's effect upon the world of art has been profound. Concepts of alienation have resulted from his cry over the dehumanization of art. Color is not spared. The theory of dehumanization is carried from Velazquez's use of light and a fixed point of view to the chiaroscurist's loss of corporeality, or separation of color and light from form. Seems to leave only the primitives and/or Ortega y Gasset with a grasp of humanity in art.

Ruskin, John. TRUE AND BEAUTIFUL. New York and Boston: H. M. Caldwell Co., (1886). 345 pp.

John Ruskin's concern for color was a constant. He had a discerning sense of aesthetics as he viewed nature. He related perception to his personal sense of wonderment which was highly moral in character. Therefore, his concept of color in painting was both moralistic and naturalistic. Quite relevant to our needs today.

Wolfflin, Heinrich. PRINCIPLES OF ART HISTORY; THE PROBLEM OF THE DEVELOPMENT OF STYLE IN LATER ART. Translated by M. D. Hottinger. New York: Dover Publications, Inc., n.d. xvi, 237 pp. Black and white illus. Paperbound.

The English translation of Heinrich Rolfflin's classic, first published in 1932, is from the seventh German edition. It includes analysis and contrast between perceived light and color in nature, and light and color as part of the conventions of an aesthetic (i.e., the artist's awareness of color reflecting from surfaces in nature but without needing an apparent equivalent in his painting). Pursues a concept that is typical Wolfflin, indulging in an ideal of the beauty of color.

Chapter 3

COLOR: ARCHITECTURE

Chapter 3

COLOR: ARCHITECTURE

Chase, Joseph Cummings. AN ARTIST TALKS ABOUT COLOR. New York: John Wiley & Sons, Inc., 1930. ix, 70 pp.

> Random thoughts and observations on color; as though in a hurry, passing by.

Kluver, Billy, et al., eds. PAVILION, BY EXPERIMENTS IN ART TECHNOLOGY. New York: E. P. Dutton and Co., Inc., 1972. xxi, 346 pp. 16 color plates, black and white illus., photos, diagrams. Bibliography. Paperbound.

> Modes and attributes of light and color are posed and juxtaposed in fascinating ways to encourage exploration of one's own environment and to develop integrated sensory responses.

Pevsner, Sir Nikolaus. STUDIES IN ART, ARCHITECTURE AND DESIGN. 2 vols. New York: Walker and Co., (c. 1968). Vol. I - FROM MANNERISM TO ROMANTICISM. 256 pp. 267 Black and white illus. Vol. II - VICTORIAN AND AFTER. 288 pp. 519 Black and white illus.

> Nikolaus Pevsner describes the different way color is used in his historical analysis of art, architecture, and design. In this well-written work, one looks forward to learning about the colors used in tapestries, carpets, glass, china, wall coverings, bookbindings, interiors of houses and institutional buildings, furniture, graphics, automobiles, and even in gardens and grounds.

Rheims, Maurice. See: COLOR: IDEOLOGY. Rheims, Maurice. THE FLOWERING OF ART NOUVEAU.

Ruskin, John. THE SEVEN LAMPS OF ARCHITECTURE. New York: Merrill and Baker, n.d. xii, 206 pp. Black and white illus.

> Ruskin's ideas of color and light in architecture are based upon his sharp visual discernment and investigation of the perception of light and shadows: the way colored materials became tools to enhance structural decoration.

Stokes, Adrian. THE IMAGE IN FORM. Ed. by Richard Wollheim. New York, Evanston, San Francisco, London: Harper & Row, Publishers, (c. 1972). 320 pp. Black and white illus. Paperbound.

This volume is a selection of writings from several of A. Stokes' works. His philosophy runs through all his work, and in this work it is presented simultaneously from different aspects. The meaning of visual luxury in architecture and art is developed into richly gratifying sensory shapes and images, using light and color, paint and stones. He describes and inspires our innermost psychological and physiological needs.

Chapter 4

COLOR: ARTISTS' CONCEPTS

Chapter 4

COLOR: ARTISTS' CONCEPTS

ALBERS, JOSEF (1888 -)

Albers, Josef. See also: COLOR: EDUCATION. Albers, Josef. INTERAC-
TION OF COLOR.

Tyler, Kenneth E. JOSEF ALBERS: WHITE LINE SQUARES. Los Angeles:
Gemini G.E.L., (c.1966). Catalog of exhibition circulated internationally by
the Los Angeles County Museum of Art. Color illus., photos. Bibliography.

> Simultaneous contrast and its seemingly unlimited possibilities is the
> subject of the WHITE LINE SQUARES. Albers is succinct in his ex-
> planation of the white line and its possibilities as a psychic and
> physical fact.

* * * * *

ANGELICO, FRA (GIOVANNI DA FIESOLE) (c. 1387/1400 - 55)

See: COLOR: IDEOLOGY. Berenson, Bernhard. ITALIAN PAINTERS OF THE
RENAISSANCE.

* * * * *

BAUDELAIRE, CHARLES PIERRE (1821 - 1867)

Baudelaire, Charles. THE PAINTER OF MODERN LIFE, AND OTHER ESSAYS.
Translated and edited by Jonathan Mayne. London, New York: Phaidon Press,
Ltd., (c. 1965). xx, 224 pp. 53 black and white illus.

> Charles Baudelaire's essay is a poetic insight into Delacroix's inves-
> tigation of color as an expression of emotions, color chemistry, and
> also the contrast between color and line. One begins to understand
> Delacroix's influence upon other artists.

* * * * *

BELLINI, GIOVANNI (c. 1430 - 1516)

See: COLOR: IDEOLOGY. Berenson, Bernhard. ITALIAN PAINTERS OF THE

17

RENAISSANCE.

* * * * *

BONNARD, PIERRE   (1867 - 1947)

*Rewald, John. PIERRE BONNARD. New York: Museum of Modern Art in collaboration with the Cleveland Museum of Art, (c. 1948). 151 pp. Color and black and white illus., photos, drawings. Paperbound.

> John Rewald writes lovingly of Bonnard, his friendship with Vuillard and the influences upon him of Japanese art and natural light (as in landscape) of Serusier and of Gauguin's color ideas. Bonnard earned the nickname of "Japanese Nabis." The study is beautifully penetrating in its analysis of his color and color decisions related to form, mass, and poetry. Fascinating that such a master of color should rely upon memory images to develop his color.

Thrall, James, et al. BONNARD AND HIS ENVIRONMENT. New York: Museum of Modern Art, (c. 1964). 116 pp. Color and black and white illus., photos. Bibliography.

> Bonnard's color theories have been clearly articulated in this monograph. His work as a colorist and his interest in combinations of unfamiliar intermediate tones are a major contribution to the painter or student of color.

*Vaillant, Annette. BONNARD. Translated by David Britt. With a dialogue between Jean Cassou and Raymond Cogniat. Commentaries by Hans R. Hahnloser. Greenwich, Conn.: New York Graphic Society, (c. 1965). 229 pp. Color and black and white illus., photos.

> At the beginning of his career, Bonnard's color was influenced by various painters such as Gauguin, Serusier, Cezanne, and Van Gogh as well as by his friends such as Ibels, Ranson, Maurice Denis, and later Vuillard and Roussel. He recognized his obsession with color and studied the effects of light upon color. The text and the breathtaking color reproductions complement each other, creating new conceptual color images of Bonnard's work.

* * * * *

BOTTICELLI, SANDRO   (1444/45 - 1510)

See: COLOR: IDEOLOGY. Berenson, Bernhard. ITALIAN PAINTERS OF THE RENAISSANCE.

* * * * *

BRAQUE, GEORGES   (1882 - 1963)

Descargues, Pierre, and Ponge, Francis. G. BRAQUE. Translated by Richard Howard and Lane Dunlop. Appreciation by Andre Malraux. New York: Harry

N. Abrams, Inc., (c. 1971). 261 pp. Color and black and white illus., photos.

> Georges Braque approached his work in solitude and with imagina-
> tion. He lived close to nature and worked out his concepts of
> color through the process of the "metier" (developing his talent
> in relation to the materials he mastered). The flavor of Braque's
> thinking permeates this study. Although the reproductions are of
> poor quality, this remains an important study.

Russell, John. G. BRAQUE. London: Phaidon Publishers, Inc., (c. 1959). 127
pp. Color and black and white illus. Bibliography.

> Braque, the colorist among the Cubists, subordinated color, to
> technique, to Cubist's design devices. Braque moved beyong as-
> serting his sense of color and subordinating design concepts. He
> tested many color concepts and experimented with new alliances,
> such as between perceived volume and color. He was influenced
> by Chardin's idea of light and visual textures. Highly informative.

* * * * *

CARAVAGGIO, MICHELANGELO DA (c. 1573/65 - 1610)

Berenson, Bernhard. CARAVAGGIO, HIS INCONGRUITY AND HIS FAME. New
York: The Macmillan Co., 1953. 122 pp. of text. 88 pp. of black and white
plates.

> Bernhard Berenson's perception of light and color in painting is
> dependent upon the artist's techniques. Berenson therefore does
> not analyze Caravaggio's color concepts. However, his descrip-
> tion of Caravaggio's color and the influence it had upon Velazquez,
> Vermeer, and Rembrandt makes this book most important.

* * * * *

CEZANNE, PAUL (1839 - 1906)

Cezanne, Paul. See: COLOR: IDEOLOGY. Venturi, Lionello. IMPRES-
SIONISTS AND SYMBOLISTS; MANET, DEGAS, MONET, PISSARRO, SISLEY,
RENOIR, CEZANNE, SEURAT, GAUGUIN, VAN GOGH, TOULOUSE-LAUTREC.

*Barnes, Albert C., and Mazia, Violette de. THE ART OF CEZANNE. Merion,
Pa.: The Barnes Foundation Press, (c. 1939). xviii, 456 pp. Black and white
illus. Catalogue data.

> Albert Barnes wrote knowingly and sensitively, yet analytically of
> Cezanne's color theories. Cezanne's arduous investigations led to
> his unique color contributions, particularly in the introduction of
> a color module (which usually was related to color planes, masses,
> and volumes), and his principles of color and light.

*Fry, Roger. CEZANNE; A STUDY OF HIS DEVELOPMENT. New York: The
Noonday Press, (c. 1958). Reprinted from the second edition by arrangement
with the Macmillan Co. 88 pp. Black and white illus. Paperbound.

Roger Fry recognized the important contribution that Cezanne made to the art world. He actually felt that it was in "the colour that Cezanne asserts most decidedly his originality and the authenticity of his gift." His book is a rich contribution to understanding Cezanne's color. Fry's vocabulary is personal, his insights are charming.

*Loran, Erle. CEZANNE'S COMPOSITION; ANALYSIS OF HIS FORM, WITH DIAGRAMS AND PHOTOGRAPHS OF HIS MOTIFS. 2nd ed. Berkeley and Los Angeles: University of California Press, (c. 1943). 141 pp. Black and white illus., photos, diagrams.

Cezanne created "light," an inner light that emanated from color relations without regard for copying realistic effects of light and shade. He was the first modern artist to be free from the servile imitation of light and shade. Cezanne's color is described and synthesized by Loran throughout this very important book.

Perruchot, Henri. CEZANNE. Translated by Humphrey Hare. Art and Destiny Series, vol. 2. Cleveland and New York: The World Publishing Co., (c. 1961). xvi, 348 pp. Black and white illus., photos. Bibliography.

The breadth of Cezanne's talent is reflected in the endless interpretations of his work and life. Henri Perruchot may overstate the influence of Pissarro with his insistence to discover "local color" as modified by light. For Cezanne that lesson was merely the beginning of his vast effect upon color in painting.

Rewald, John. PAUL CEZANNE. Translated by Margaret H. Liebman. London: Spring Books, 1950, 1959, 1965. xvi, 205 pp. Mostly black and white illus. Bibliography.

John Rewald's sensitive biography of Cezanne includes a penetrating grasp of Cezanne's involvement with light and color in nature which led to his profound color ideas that have influenced all contemporary art.

*_____, ed. PAUL CEZANNE LETTERS. Translated by Marguerite Kay. Oxford: Bruno Cassirer, Ltd., 1941, 1944, 1946. 306 pp. Black and white illus., photos.

Cezanne's letters are important to the student of color, for they reflect the constant awareness of illumination and surface colors in daily thought that led to his role as father of Modern Art and as one of the great colorists. The letters to Emile Bernard in particular deal with ideas of half-tone, quarter tones, and color in optical color sensations.

*Schapiro, Meyer. PAUL CEZANNE. 2nd ed. The Library of Great Painters Series. New York: Harry N. Abrams, Inc., 1962, (c. 1952). 126 pp. Mostly color illus.

Meyer Schapiro discusses the effect of nature upon Cezanne's color, compares Cezanne's interpretation of color in nature to Monet's, and contrasts their concepts of light. He also describes the development of Cezanne's color by citing examples in his work, and traces the effects of his techniques upon abstract art.

* * * * *

CHARDIN, JEAN BAPTISTE SIMEON   (1699 - 1779)

de la Mare, Walter. CHARDIN, (1699-1779). London: Faber & Faber, Ltd., n.d. 24 pp. 10 color plates.

Walter de la Mare's literary analysis of the work of Chardin places Chardin within the sphere of influence of his time, but singles out the uniqueness of his ability to achieve deeper meaning through his use of light as subject in painting. We appreciate Chardin's effects of light more as a result of de la Mare's beautiful study.

Denvir, Bernard. CHARDIN. New York: Harper & Brothers Publishers, 1950. 16 pp. 39 plates (part color). Bibliography.

Bernard Denvir understood Chardin as a painter of light and forerunner of Corot, Monet, the Impressionists and Cezanne. He discusses Chardin's use of the alchemy of color and the complexities existing in his unity of color. A little too sparse.

Wildenstein, Georges. CHARDIN. Revised, enlarged, and translated by Stuart Gilbert. Greenwich, Conn.: New York Graphic Society, Ltd., 1969 (c. 1963). 276 pp. Color and black and white illus. Bibliography.

The influences upon Chardin, his contributions to the art of the still life, and especially the description of his achievements in light and color effects are described carefully. The plates reflect best of all the artists's aspirations and chromatic-tonal color concepts, his ability to create color effects and color harmonies.

* * * * *

CORREGGIO (ANTONIO ALLEGRI)   (c. 1494 - 1534)

See: COLOR: IDEOLOGY. Berenson, Bernhard. ITALIAN PAINTERS OF THE RENAISSANCE.

See also: COLOR: PALETTES. Eastlake, Sir Charles Lock. METHODS AND MATERIALS OF PAINTING OF THE GREAT SCHOOLS AND MASTERS, vols. 1 & 2.

* * * * *

DAVIS, STUART   (1894 - 1964)

Goossen, E. C. STUART DAVIS. The Great American Artists Series. New York: George Braziller, Inc., (c. 1959). (Distributed by Pocket Books, Inc.) 128 pp. Mostly color plates. Paperbound.

Important American painter whose painting relates first to color, rather than form, mass, or shape. Stuart Davis' paintings represent an important step toward pure color usage in this country and Goosen writes knowledgably about his usage of color.

* * * * *

DEGAS, HILAIRE GERMAIN EDGAR (1834 - 1917)

Huttinger, Edouard. DEGAS. Translated by Ellen Healy. The Q.L.P. Series. New York: Crown Publishers, Inc., 1960. 92 pp. Color and black and white illus. Bibliography.

Important monograph on Degas. Covers nearly every aspect of his life and work, but only touches upon his color theories. However, useful because of Degas' contributions. Tantalizing, although all too brief.

* * * * *

DELACROIX (FERDINAND VICTOR) EUGENE (1798 - 1863)

*Baudelaire, Charles. DELACROIX, HIS LIFE AND WORK. New York: Lear Publishers, (c. 1947). 94 pp. Mostly black and white illus.

Baudelaire's "homage" to Delacroix is in itself a poetic color study, to be grasped as metaphor, especially when he described the "as if-afternoon color of Veronese" in reference to Delacroix's work. Touches upon Delacroix's curiosity comparing it to Leonardo's, for the chemistry of color and his conversations with manufacturers of color. Baudelaire quotes freely from Delacroix's conversations and his journals, in which Delacroix relates color to mathematics and music. All helpful to the student of color.

Delacroix, Eugene. THE JOURNAL OF EUGENE DELACROIX. Translated by Walter Pach. New York: Grove Press, Inc., 1961, (c. 1937 by Covici, Friede, Inc., 1948 by Crown Publishers). 750 pp. Black and white illus. Paperbound.

Eugene Delacroix's writings include many perceptions of light and color in nature, organized by his highly analytical and imaginative eye into a tantalizing verbal picture. His ideas have been inspirational to many painters. He writes of many painters with acute insight and is particularly instructive about their use of color.

* * * * *

DELAUNAY, SONIA (1885 -   )

*Damase, Jacques. SONIA DELAUNAY RHYTHMS AND COLOURS. Preface by Michel Hoog. Greenwich, Conn.: New York Graphic Society, Ltd., (c. 1972). 412 pp. Color and black and white illus.

Robert and Sonia Delaunay aspired to develop their ideas of color

(color rhythm, light, and color) to pervade all familiar forms of everyday life. They believed in color as a sensuous element, and claimed that the senses were reality. This beautiful book presents their color theories and also contains many lovely color reproductions of their paintings, as well as Sonia Delaunay's furniture, fabric, and clothing designs.

* * * * *

DERAIN, ANDRE (1880 - 1954)

Sutton, Denys. ANDRE DERAIN. London: Phaidon Publishers, Inc., (c. 1959). 158 pp. Mostly black and white illus. Bibliography.

A psychological study of Andre Derain as a man and as an artist; his ideas, influences, and artistic development. Denys Sutton traces Derain's path from Fauvism to his interests in several styles and periods, touching upon his interest in many color theories which led to his own eclecticism. Sutton supports the argument that a strong tradition is necessary to an artist's originality.

* * * * *

DOVE, ARTHUR GARFIELD (1880 - 1946)

*Wight, Frederick S. ARTHUR G. DOVE. Berkeley and Los Angeles: University of California Press, (c. 1958). 96 pp. Illus. (part color), photos. Bibliography.

Arthur Dove's theories lead to the art of pure color and form. Color expression, color symbolism, and color significance form the nucleus of his ideas. Charming.

* * * * *

FRAGONARD, JEAN HONORE (1732 - 1806)

*Thuillier, Jacques. FRAGONARD; BIOGRAPHICAL AND CRITICAL STUDY. Translated by Robert Allen. Geneva: Editions d'Art Albert Skira, (c. 1967). 156 pp. Color illus. Bibliography.

According to Thuillier, Fragonard uses color to explore the space and dynamic relationships that occupy the depth of the visible scene. Thuillier makes interesting color associations among the ideas of Fragonard and Rubens, Titian, Tintoretto, and Boucher. Refreshing monograph and pleasant color insights.

* * * * *

GIOTTO, DI BONDONE (c. 1266/67 - 1337)

See: COLOR: IDEOLOGY. Berenson, Bernhard. ITALIAN PAINTERS OF THE RENAISSANCE.

GOYA, Y LUCIENTES, FRANCISCO JOSE DE (1746 - 1828)

Gudiol, Jose. FRANCISCO DE GOYA Y LUCIENTES GOYA. Translated by
Priscilla Muller. The Library of Great Painters Series. New York: Harry N.
Abrams, Inc., n.d. 168 pp. Color and black and white illus.

> Francisco Goya's technique, how it developed relating to his per-
> ception of light in balance with objects, is carefully described and
> documented. The psychological development of his palette (colors
> related to his personal needs of expression) is described and related
> to events, such as his loneliness, in a fascinating although too
> brief manner.

* * * * *

HOFMANN, HANS (1880 - 1966)

See also: COLOR: IDEOLOGY. Hess, Thomas B., and Ashbery, John, eds.
LIGHT, FROM ATEN TO LASER.

*Hofmann, Hans. SEARCH FOR THE REAL AND OTHER ESSAYS. Edited by
Sarah T. Weeks and Bartlett H. Hayes, Jr. Andover, Mass.: The Addison
Gallery of American Art, (c. 1948). 78 pp. 1 color, black and white illus.,
photos, diagrams.

> Hans Hofmann's color theories are highly personal. He touches upon
> scientific phenomena in a lyrical and intuitive way; as a process in
> discovering rather than information learned from an exterior source.
> As with his teaching and paintings, his book offers a fresh point of
> view on color.

* * * * *

HOPPER, EDWARD (1882 - 1967)

Goodrich, Lloyd. EDWARD HOPPER. New York: Harry N. Abrams, Inc.,
n.d. 306 pp. Color and black and white illus. Bibliography.

> Lloyd Goodrich presents clues to the color reality of Edward
> Hopper's world, primarily by technical descriptions of his methods
> for achieving luminosity in etchings, watercolors, and paintings.
> The color plates are beautiful. The visual texture differences
> achieved between a drawing and etching are especially fascinat-
> ing.

* * * * *

KANDINSKY, WASSILY (1886 - 1944)

See also: COLOR: PSYCHOLOGY. Kandinsky, Wassily. CONCERNING THE
SPIRITUAL IN ART, AND PAINTING IN PARTICULAR, 1912.

*Grohmann, Will. WASSILY KANDINSKY, LIFE AND WORK. Translated by
Norbert Guterman. New York: Harry N. Abrams, Inc., n.d. 428 pp.

Color and black and white illus., photos. Bibliography.

> Will Grohmann analyzes the influences and effects of music,
> mysticism, and nature upon the art of Kandinsky. He traces
> the way Kandinsky used color related to his pursuit of the
> inner core of nature and the sources of life. A beautiful
> study.

Kandinsky, Wassily, and Rebay, Hilla, eds. POINT AND LINE TO PLANE;
CONTRIBUTION TO THE ANALYSIS OF PICTORIAL ELEMENTS. Translated
by Howard Dearstyne and Hilla Rebay. New York: Solomon R. Guggenheim
Foundation for the Museum of Non-Objective Painting, 1947. 196 pp. Illus.,
diagrams.

> Although color is not dealt with as concept, the principles of
> design in line, point, and plane are directly related and basic
> to Kandinsky's color theories.

*Read, [Sir] Herbert [Edward]. KANDINSKY (1866 - 1944). R. H. Wilenski,
ed. Introduction by Herbert Read. New York: George Wittenborn, (c. 1959
by Faber & Faber, Ltd.). 24 pp. 8 color plates, black and white illus.

> Kandinsky, through his experimentation at the extreme end of
> Fauvism, was among those who began investigating color for
> its symbolic overtones without representation in visual commu-
> nication. He felt an inherent underlying abstract structure in
> art that was similar to the structure and order in music. Herbert
> Read's introduction to the thoughts of Kandinsky in this mono-
> graph are important and delightful.

* * * * *

KLEE, PAUL (1879 - 1940)

Di San Lazzaro, Gualtieri. KLEE: A STUDY OF HIS LIFE AND WORK. Translated by Stuart Hood. New York: Frederick A. Praeger, Inc., (c. 1957).
2nd ed., 1964. 304 pp. Illus. (part color). Biographical notes. Catalogue
of principal works. Bibliography.

> One of the numerous efforts to interpret Klee's writings. Fortunate-
> ly, the book is filled with abundant quotations about Klee's percep-
> tion of color and light, psychological insights about color, and
> color notations. Helpful to those who prefer digested words to the
> original.

Haftmann, Werner. THE MIND AND WORK OF PAUL KLEE. New York:
Frederick A. Praeger, Inc., 1967. 213 pp. Illus. (part color).

> Werner Haftmann's biography of Paul Klee documents the in-
> fluences upon his life and art. He writes brilliantly of Klee's
> pursual of light phenomena through his painting. Unfortunately,
> he applies acceptable conventional color vocabulary to his anal
> ysis of color, i.e., dark-color to warm-light. Klee's intention
> to find the equivocation to musical notation is diminished. The
> book is helpful as a bridge for those who prefer the concrete to

the metaphor.

*Klee, Felix, ed. THE DIARIES OF PAUL KLEE, 1898 - 1918. Berkeley and Los Angeles: University of California Press, (c. 1964). xx, 424 pp. Black and white illus., photos. Paperbound.

> Klee anguished more about color than line and felt often that his color results bore little fruit compared to his anguishing. His journals relate to his color theories even when he is discussing other things, for Klee was of such a fibre that all aspects of his life reflected light and color.

*Klee, Paul. ON MODERN ART. Introduction by Herbert Read. Translated by Paul Findley. London: Faber & Faber, Ltd., n.d. 55 pp. Black and white illus.

> Klee gives a broader definition to chiaroscuro, taking it out of the realm of the technical into the realm of the poetic. His color theories begin with an abstract idea of the quality of color, or color as quality. He relates color to expression and defines basic laws for developing quality and/or expression.

*_____. PEDAGOGICAL SKETCHBOOK. Translation and introduction by Sibyl Moholy-Nagy. New York: Frederick A. Praeger, (c. 1953). 60 pp. Black and white illus.

> This book by Paul Klee was first published under the title: PADAGOGISCHES SKIZZENBUCH 1925, as the second of the fourteen Bauhaus books edited by Walter Gropius and L. Moholy-Nagy.

> As Leonardo or Goethe, Klee found that interaction or mutual support as a concept in nature was basic to his art theories. With diagrams he expresses the need for color not only "to move there" but to be "everywhere" and also "there."

*Lynton, Norbert. KLEE. London: Spring Books, (c. 1964). 43 pp. 49 color plates. Black and white illus.

> The monograph draws primarily from Klee's journal for insight. "Color keyboard of my watercolors pots," introduced the poetic way Klee approaches the notations of his color ideas. He closely aligns the doing, the technique of invention, to perception and his uniquely expressive color theories. His journals include descriptions of insights into color mixes in light and pigment. His reference to music is constant.

* * * * *

KNATHS, KARL (1891 - 1971)

Mocsanyi, Paul. KARL KNATHS. Introduction by Duncan Phillips, appreciation by Emanuel Benson. Washington: The Phillips Gallery, (c. 1957). 101 pp. Illus. (part color).

Karl Knaths' very American use of color relates in theory rather than practice to the color ideas of the Cubists. But spiritually and visually it relates to the concepts of purity in personal expression developed by John Marin, Marsden Hartley, and Arthur Dove. In the introduction, Duncan Phillips relates Karl Knaths' work and color to that of Georges Braque.

* * * * *

LEONARDO DA VINCI (1452 - 1519)

See also: COLOR: IDEOLOGY. Berenson, Bernhard. ITALIAN PAINTERS OF THE RENAISSANCE. COLOR: PALETTES. Eastlake, Sir Charles Lock. METHODS AND MATERIALS OF PAINTING OF THE GREAT SCHOOLS AND MASTERS, vols. 1 & 2.

Goldscheider, Ludwig. LEONARDO DA VINCI: THE ARTIST. 3rd ed. London: Phaidon Press; New York: Oxford University Press, 1948. 44 pp. Mostly black and white illus., map. Bibliography.

Many of the notes by Goldscheider, as well as the biography by Vasari in the publication, discuss Leonardo's concern with light and shadow. Leonardo's interest in nature studies, his studies of color and of the color and light effects in nature, as well as the relationship of his studies to his paintings are presented. It is a good source for a beginning in understanding the levels of meaning attached to the visual metaphor using light and shadow as the vehicle for expression in art.

*Leonardo da Vinci. A TREATISE ON PAINTING. Translated by John Francis Rigaud. London: George Bell & Sons, 1892. lxvii, 238 pp. Illus., diagrams.

Colors and coloring is a particularly rewarding section as Leonardo records his own impressions so faithfully, and the breadth of his observations and methodology in thinking is so beautifully ordered. He wrote of the various modes of appearance and attributes of light and color before such nomenclature and organization had been considered. He analyzed the colors in shadows and speculated upon changes and wrestled with the concept of white as a non-color.

* * * * *

LOUIS, MORRIS (1912 - 1962)

See also: COLOR: IDEOLOGY. Hess, Thomas B., and Ashbery, John, eds. LIGHT, FROM ATEN TO LASER.

Fried, Michael. MORRIS LOUIS. New York: Harry N. Abrams, Inc., Publishers, n.d. 220 pp. Color and black and white illus., photo. Bibliography.

Morris Louis' color is analyzed here by Michael Fried who traces influences upon Louis' work by such people as Jackson Pollock and Helen Frankenthaler. He pays particular attention to the technique of thin veils of color. The book is lovely to look at, yet as with the work of many of the contemporary color painters, no one has crystalized or developed their results into meaningful concepts.

_____. MORRIS LOUIS 1912 - 1962. Boston: Museum of Fine Arts, 1967. 82 pp. Color and black and white plates. Notes. Bibliography.

A monograph of Morris Louis. Color becomes the picture, its own meaning and its own theory, perhaps to be comprehended visually for the time being rather than clearly articulated verbally!

* * * * *

MACDONALD-WRIGHT, STANTON (1890 -   )

*MacDonald-Wright, Stanton. THE ART OF STANTON MACDONALD-WRIGHT. Introduction by David W. Scott. Washington: Smithsonian Press, 1967. 100 pp. Color and black and white illus. Includes "A Treatise on Color."

The treatise on color by MacDonald-Wright is one of the most informative, most imaginative, and most instructive for a painter interested in color. Although the study is brief, the contents include historical information, his opinions upon previous color theories, and his own quite fascinating theory of color harmony and contrast.

* * * * *

MALEVICH, KASIMIR S. (1878 - 1935)

Malevich, K. S. ESSAYS ON ART 1915 - 1933. Vol. 1. Translated by Xenia Glowacki-Prus and Arnold McMilljn. Chester Springs, PA.: Du Four Editions, Inc., (c. 1968). 48 black and white plates, illus.

Kasimir Malevich's essays embody an approach to analysis that offers a sharp contrast to the typically scientific. However, his writings reveal a deep awareness of contemporary art. Color ideas are to be gleaned from his writings, and the effort is worthwhile. Malevich's theories relate color to the material and composition rather than to an aesthetic. He includes the Russian approach to Futurism, Constructivism, and Suprematism.

* * * * *

MARIN, JOHN (c. 1872/75 - 1953)

Helm, MacKinley. JOHN MARIN. Boston: Institute of Contemporary Art, (c. 1948). 255 pp. Mostly black and white illus.

John Marin's color is investigated, and his highly individualistic and lyrical color theory is developed.

MATISSE, HENRI (1869 - 1954)

*Barnes, Albert C., and Mazia, Violette de. THE ART OF HENRI MATISSE.
Marion, Pa.: The Barnes Foundation Press, (c. 1933, 1959). xvi, 464 pp.
Black and white illus. Biographical sketch.

> Albert Barnes and Violette de Mazia wrote just before the current
> wave of behavioral psychology and its explanations for most of
> what we do. As a result, their psychological and philosophical
> explanations of why we do things have a pleasant, old-fashioned
> ring. Their comprehension of color influences upon Matisse's
> work is superb, and they write in glowing, verbal images of his
> development. Current colorists may find interesting comparisons
> to make between the authors' views of Matisse's "bands of colors,"
> his use of stripes, and bare canvas, to Josef Albers' or Kenneth
> Noland's studies. The analyses of Matisse's paintings are filled
> with color descriptions and are most stimulating.

*Barr, Alfred H., Jr. MATISSE, HIS ART AND HIS PUBLIC. New York: The
Museum of Modern Art, (c. 1951). 591 pp. Mostly black and white illus.,
photos, drawings. Bibliography.

> Matisse's conceptual and artistic revolution had dramatic effects
> upon contemporary art. Alfred Barr chronologically traces the
> influences upon Matisse by Gustave Moreau, Paul Cezanne, and
> other elders. He traces Matisse's influence upon the Fauves,
> the Impressionists, Neo-Impressionists, and Pointilists. He follows
> Matisse's unique development through his color harmonies in blues
> and reds, his involvement in relating dance and music to his paint-
> ings and color studies. Alfred Barr also recognizes the profound
> effect that his travels in Spain and Morocco had upon Matisse's
> use and love of color. A beautiful and rewarding study.

*Frey, Roger. HENRI MATISSE. New York: E. Weyhe, (c. 1935). 24 pp.
3 color plates, 60 black and white plates, 7 drawings.

> Roger Fry is acute in his observations of Matisse's torment and in-
> spiration caused by the equivocal nature of painting, by the com-
> plexities of the qualities of form plus tone, color, and the influence
> of the luminous atmosphere with which perceived space is filled.
> He feels that Matisse follows Caravaggio, Monet, Rembrandt, and
> Cezanne in his color and design ("plastic") importance, and contri-
> bution to art.

* * * * *

MOHOLY-NAGY, LASZLO (LADISLAUS) (1895 - 1946)

Moholy-Nagy, Laszlo. THE NEW VISION AND ABSTRACT OF AN ARTIST.
4th ed., rev. New York: Wittenborn, 1947, (1928). 92 pp. Illus.

> Laszlo Moholy-Nagy aspired to the conquest of space and dis-
> covered that light was the way to comprehend and conquer it.

He used light to expand the boundaries of painting, to the point of attempting new technical means to achieve greater intensity of light. Important historical document.

* * * * *

MONDRIAN, PIET (1872 - 1944)

Tomassoni, Italo. MONDRIAN. London, New York, Sydney, Toronto: Hamlyn Publishing Group, Ltd., (c. 1970). Distributed in the United States of America by Crown Publishiers, Inc. 96 pp. 47 color illus. 32 black and white illus.

The need for rational order, a desire to resolve the problems of technology and to admit its reality in order to create an equilibrium between the individual and the universe were basic concerns to Mondrian in the development of his art. Color was conceived "plastically" or as part of his "morphoplasticism." His thinking is articulated logically and clearly.

* * * * *

MONET, CLAUDE (1840 - 1926)

See also: COLOR: IDEOLOGY. Venturi, Lionello. IMPRESSIONISTS AND SYMBOLISTS; MANET, DEGAS, MONET, PISSARRO, SISLEY, RENOIR, CEZANNE, SEURAT, GAUGUIN, VAN GOGH, TOULOUSE-LAUTREC.

Seitz, William C. CLAUDE MONET. The Library of Great Painters Series. New York: Harry N. Abrams, Inc., n.d. 158 pp. 132 illus. 48 color plates, photos. Bibliography.

William Seitz poses possible kinds of color questions which Monet may have asked of himself in developing his color theories and techniques. The writer studied Monet's paintings for visual understanding of the color sensation, perception, design, and time of day qualities that evolved into the shapes and techniques which we identify as Monet's unique contributions. The black and white plates compared to black and white photographs of particular scenes are most interesting and suggest more development of form and mass than one usually associates with Monet.

* _____. CLAUDE MONET, SEASONS AND MOMENTS. New York: Museum of Modern Art, 1960. 64 pp. Color and black and white illus., photos. Bibliography.

William Seitz writes glowingly of Monet's involvement and effort to transform objects into the various attributes of light and color, such as sparkle, glow, and shimmer. Monet moved naturalism to its bursting point, to the moment of the "Impressionist's Eye," and later one sees the possibility for the advent of the Fauves.

Taillandier, Yvon. CLAUDE MONET. Translated by A. P. H. Hamilton. The Q.L.P. Art Series. New York: Crown Publishers, Inc., n.d. 94 pp. Color and black and white illus. Biography. Bibliography.

Unfortunately, poorly written, but fascinating accounts of Monet watching sun, fog, mist, and water. Traces Monet's thoughts and the sources that influenced his innermost impressions such as Japanese art and philosophy.

* * * * *

NEWMAN, BARNETT (1905 - 1970)

*Hess, Thomas B. BARNETT NEWMAN. New York: The Museum of Modern Art, (c. 1971). Distributed by New York Graphic Society, Ltd., Greenwich, Conn. 158 pp. Color and black and white illus., photos. Bibliography.

Thomas Hess' book on the work of Barnett Newman is most pleasant reading. Color is treated as an element of painting and pigment, and as a strong spiritual force.

* * * * *

NOLAND, KENNETH C. (1924 -   )

See: COLOR: IDEOLOGY. Hess, Thomas B., and Ashbery, John, Eds. LIGHT, FROM ATEN TO LASER.

* * * * *

OZENFANT, AMEDEE (1886 - 1966)

Ozenfant, Amedee. FOUNDATIONS OF MODERN ART. Translated by John Rodker. New York: Dover Publications, Inc., (c. 1952). (First German edition 1931, first French edition 1928, first English edition 1931, first American edition 1931. Part I - The balance sheet: writing, painting, sculpture, architecture, music, science, religion, philosophy. Part II - Structures for a new spirit.) xviii, 348 pp. Black and white illus., photos, tables. Paperbound.

Amedee Ozenfant's creative and logical mind took an emotional turn when dealing with what he did not like. His open dislike of Cezanne and the Fauves serves as the basis for his own tonal system of color theory. His writings are still inspirational.

* * * * *

PERUGINO (PIETRO DI CRISTOFORO VANNUCCI) (c. 1445/50 - 1523)

See: COLOR: PALETTES. Eastlake, Sir Charles Lock. METHODS AND MATERIALS OF PAINTING OF THE GREAT SCHOOLS AND MASTERS, vols. 1 & 2.

* * * * *

PISSARRO, CAMILLE (c. 1830 - 1903)

See also: COLOR: IDEOLOGY. Venturi, Lionello. IMPRESSIONISTS AND SYMBOLISTS; MANET, DEGAS, MONET, PISSARRO, SISLEY, RENOIR, CEZANNE, SEURAT, GAUGUIN, VAN GOGH, TOULOUSE-LAUTREC.

Pissarro, Camille. CAMILLE PISSARRO: LETTERS TO HIS SON LUCIEN. Edited with the assistance of Lucien Pissarro by John Rewald. New York: Pantheon Books Inc., (c. 1943). 367 pp. 90 black and white illus.

> Camille Pissarro's letters to his son are filled with affection and are also highly educational. Pissarro, in his desire to bridge the physical gap between himself and his son, wrote with endless patience of his painterly efforts, his interest in color, color theories, and particular perceptual color problems.

* * * * *

RAPHAEL (RAFFAELLO SANTI) (1483 - 1520)

See: COLOR: IDEOLOGY. Berenson, Bernhard. ITALIAN PAINTERS OF THE RENAISSANCE.

See also: COLOR PALETTES. Eastlake, Sir Charles Lock. METHODS AND MATERIALS OF PAINTING OF THE GREAT SCHOOLS AND MASTERS, vols. 1 & 2.

* * * * *

REMBRANDT (REMBRADT VAN HARMENSZ RIJN) (1606 - 1669)

*Gerson, Horst. REMBRANDT PAINTINGS. Translated by Heinz Norden. New York: William Morrow and Co. Inc., (c. 1968). 527 pp. Color and black and white illus. Bibliography.

> Horst Gerson writes analytically but does not sacrifice the sense of drama in Rembrandt's art and life. He describes carefully the relationship between the brush mark and concept, between the techniques and the powerful quality of light achieved in paintings, drawings, and etchings. He carefully traces light, color, and design through the development of the artist's life.

Goldscheider, Ludwig, ed. REMBRANDT: PAINTINGS, DRAWINGS AND ETCHINGS. Introduction by Henri Focillon. London: Phaidon Press, Ltd., 1964, (c. 1960). 207 pp. Color and black and white illus.

> An excellent and sensitive guide to the personal world of Rembrandt in his pursuit of light intensified by entirely new kinds of light perception and his use of chiaroscuro. Henri Focillons hints at Rembrandt's new system of tonality in dealing with light concepts carried to his techniques in painting and etching.

* * * * *

REINHARDT, AD (1913 - 1967)

See: COLOR: IDEOLOGY. Hess, Thomas B., and Ashbery, John, eds. LIGHT, FROM ATEN TO LASER.

* * * * *

RENOIR, PIERRE AUGUSTE (1841 - 1919)

See also: COLOR: IDEOLOGY. Venturi, Lionello. IMPRESSIONISTS AND SYMBOLISTS.

*Barnes, Albert C., and Mazia, Violette de. THE ART OF RENOIR. Foreword by John Dewey. Merion, Pa.: The Barnes Foundation Press, (c. 1935). xv, 515 pp. Black and white illus.

> Excellent source for study of Renoir's development in his color perception and color use. Barnes describes the supremacy of color, with predominance of rose-red, leading to color suffusion. He traces the influences of traditional color and light upon Renoir, and pays particular attention to flesh-painting and the painting of textiles.

* * * * *

REYNOLDS, SIR JOSHUA (1723 - 1792)

*Reynolds, Sir Joshua. DISCOURSES ON ART, WITH SELECTIONS FROM THE IDLER. Edited by Stephen O. Mitchell. Indianapolis: Bobbs-Merrill, (1965). xxxviii, 252 pp. Illus., portraits. Bibliography.

> Sir Joshua Reynolds' advice on the art of coloring includes possibilities of studying old masters, copying great paintings, and observing nature. His eighteenth century warnings to develop originality from concepts is most pertinent today.

* * * * *

RUBENS, SIR PETER PAUL (1577 - 1640)

Burckhardt, Jakob. RUBENS. London: Phaidon Press, Ltd., (1950). xi. 249 pp. 140 illus. (4 color). Bibliography.

> Jakob Burckhardt describes Rubens' youthful encounter with the work and style of Caravaggio as personnally overwhelming for Rubens. He discusses the other sources of color influence as well. He analyzes Rubens' ability to develop sensuous color that remains oddly moral.

Cabanne, Pierre. RUBENS. Translated by Oliver Bernard. New York: Tudor Publishing Co., (c. 1967). 286 pp. Color and black and white illus.

> Rubens' remarkable ability to handle color is carefully described in detail by Pierre Cabanne, who analyzes his paintings one by one. He often quotes authorities, sometimes of Ruben's day, as well as later art critics and historians.

*Van Puyvelde, Leo. THE SKETCHES OF RUBENS. Translated by Eveline Winkworth. New York: The Beechhurst Press, 1951, 1954. 97 pp. 104 pp. of of black and white illus. Catalogue raisonne of the sketches reproduced.

Color is discussed throughout this remarkable book, and a separate
chapter of color analysis relates the beauty of Rubens' color to his
technique in painting and to the emotional intention of each work.
He discusses Rubens' use of juxtaposition and the new diffused lighting
present in his mature period. Rubens observed the effects of light and
color directly in nature. Van Puyvelde makes a direct correlation between the Christian Humanism and belief in Stoicism of the time, to
Ruben's intellectual freedom and sense of purpose. He organized each
and every tone of color, every subtle shade, and fugitive light. Van
Puyvelde analyzes the different color effects and changes of illumination in sketches developed into final works.

* * * * *

SARGENT, JOHN SINGER   (1856 - 1925)

Hoopes, Donelson F.   THE PRIVATE WORLD OF JOHN SINGER SARGENT.
Foreword by Hermann Warner Williams, Jr.   Plainview, N.Y.:   Shorewood Publishers, Inc., (c. 1964).   (Catalogue of the Exhibition for the Corcoran Gallery
of Art, The Cleveland Museum of Art, Worchester Art Museum, Munson-
Williams-Proctor Institute.)   illus. (part color).   Bibliography.

John Sargent's color theories move beyond Impressionism and set the
way for a new realism. The monograph merely touches upon the theories he used in his paintings.

* * * * *

SEURAT, GEORGES PIERRE (1859 - 1891)

See also: COLOR: IDEOLOGY. Venturi, Lionello. IMPRESSIONISTS AND
SYMBOLISTS: MANET, DEGAS, MONET, PISSARRO, SISLEY, RENOIR, CEZANNE,
SEURAT, GAUGUIN, VAN GOGH, TOULOUSE-LAUTREC.

Courthion, Pierre.   GEORGES SEURAT.   Translated by Norbert Guterman.   New
York: Harry N. Abrams, Inc., n.d.   160 pp.   Color and black and white illus.
Bibliography.

A pleasant history of the sources and influences of Seurat's color theories.

*Homer, William Innes.   SEURAT AND THE SCIENCE OF PAINTING.   Cam-
bridge: The M.I.T. Press, (c. 1964).   xvi, 327 pp.   Illus. (part color),
diagrams.   Bibliography.

A study of Seurat's concept of light and color as observed in his
drawings, paintings, and writings related to the contemporary scientific theories. The research is excellent and the synthesis of ideas from
source influences is fascinating. Sutter, Ogden Rood, Chevreul, Blanc,
and Delacroix are among the specific influences analyzed. Seurat's
sensibility and uniqueness are treated with deep insight and sensitivity.

*Rewald, John.   GEORGES SEURAT.   2nd ed.   Revised, enlarged, and translated by

Lionel Abel. New York: Wittenborn & Co., (c. 1943, 1946). xx, 125 pp.
Mostly black and white illus. Notes, bibliography.

> Rewald's prose echoes the patience and brilliance of Seurat's "tiny
> multi-colored strokes. . .which gave it that intense life and lumi-
> nostiy which are the secret of his style." He tells us specifically
> of Seurat's color investigations, the friends who influenced him, as
> well as the many sources of scientific influrence of the day.

Russell, John. SEURAT. New York, Washington: Frederick A. Praeger, Inc.,
(c. 1965). 286 pp. Illus. (part color). Bibliography. Paperbound.

> John Russell's biography traces the influences of Seurat's parents,
> various specific neighborhoods and environments upon his aesthetic
> development. He documents drawings and paintings related to
> activities and discoveries, such as seventy-two hours of watching
> light or portrayal of the circus. Russell provides endless detail
> in an absorbing if not inspirational manner.

* * * * *

TINTORETTO, JACOPO (1518 - 1594)

See: COLOR: IDEOLOGY. Berenson, Bernhard. ITALIAN PAINTERS OF THE
RENAISSANCE.

* * * * *

TITIAN (TIZIANO VECELLIO) (1487/90 - 1576)

See: COLOR: IDEOLOGY. Berenson, Bernhard. ITALIAN PAINTERS OF THE
RENAISSANCE.

See also: COLOR: PALETTES. Eastlake, Sir Charles Lock. METHODS AND
MATERIALS OF PAINTING OF THE GREAT SCHOOLS AND MASTERS, vols.
1 & 2.

* * * * *

TURNER, JOSEPH (1775 - 1851)

Butlin, Martin. TURNER, WATERCOLOURS. New York: Watson-Guptill Publications, (1928). 82 pp. 32 color plates. Bibliography.

> Turner used water color as atmospheric perspective to draw the eye
> into depth, to catch sensations of light upon water, and to develop
> vivid textures. Martin Butlin observes Turner's work keenly and
> writes unconventionally, including notes about Turner's finger paint-
> ing as part of his world of color.

*Gage, John. COLOR IN TURNER; POETRY AND TRUTH. New York, Washington: Frederick A. Praeger, Publishers, (c. 1969). 285 pp. Color and black and white illus. Bibliography.

> Brilliant documentation of Turner's color theories in spite of his distrust for same. Turner's analysis of color in the paintings of old masters largely inspired his concepts. John Gage traces the development of Turner's complex and comprehensive body of aesthetic theory, as well as the influences of friends and groups such as the Monro Circle.

* _____. TURNER: RAIN, STEAM AND SPEED. New York: The Viking Press, Inc., (c. 1972). 99 pp. Black and white illus.

> A clear analysis of the realistic and poetic light and color effects created by minimal color and an extraordinary technical virtuosity is presented in John Gage's book on Turner's paintings.

*Gowing, Lawrence. TURNER: IMAGINATION AND REALITY. New York: The Museum of Modern Art, (1966). Distributed by Doubleday & Co., Inc. 64 pp. Color and black and white illus. Bibliography.

> Paint existed as a color reality for Turner rather than as light and color in nature or science. He was aware of Newton's prismatic colors, but approached the rainbow as a subject through poetry rather than science. Lawrence Gowing's analysis of Turner's color is inspiring.

* * * * *

VAN EYCK, JAN (1380/90 - 1440)

See: COLOR: PALETTES. Eastlake, Sir Charles Lock. METHODS AND MATERIALS OF PAINTING OF THE GREAT SCHOOLS AND MASTERS, vols. 1 & 2.

* * * * *

VAN GOGH, VINCENT (1853 - 1890)

*Stone, Irving and Jean, eds. DEAR THEO; THE AUTOBIOGRAPHY. New York: Grove Press, Inc., 1960 (c. 1937). (Edition is published by arrangement with Doubleday & Co., Inc.) 572 pp. Black and white illus. Paperbound.

> The letters to his brother are among the beautiful and poignant records of an artist's effort to record his struggle to "see" light, color, and forms in nature. Van Gogh writes of his attempts to use watercolors and to maintain transparency controls as an equivalent to additive mixes. His obsession with capturing the colors of green, and his recognition of the power of color as a mystical force are equal to his sensitivity for using materials in a personal way to achieve color effects. He documents his concern with studying color as used by other artists such as Rembrandt and Hals and their interpretation of light and color in nature.

* * * * *

VASARELY, VICTOR (1908 -   )

*Spies, Werner. VASARELY. New York: Harry N. Abrams, Inc., n.d.
Distributed by World Publishing Co., New York. 76 pp. Color and black
and white illus. Biography. Bibliography. Paperbound.

> The relationship of color to Vasarely's concepts of plastic qualities,
> optical art, as well as the role of color in his artistic development,
> are nicely drawn by Werner Spies.

*_____. VICTOR VASARELY. Translated by Robert Erich Wolf. New York:
Harry N. Abrams, Inc., (c. 1971). 205 pp. Color and black and white
illus., photos. Bibliography.

> Spies writes carefully of a new compositional principle, "the
> serially variable assemblage of our aesthetic perceptual image."
> Vasarely's system of visual perception has roots in the work of
> Seurat and Malevitch and the ideas of the Impressionists and Cu-
> bists. There is a remarkable shift from tradition in relating intel-
> lectual relationships and reassigning of artistic ancestors. Spies
> presents a detailed description of psycho-physiological imbalances
> and how to achieve them. Vasarely depends upon color to pro-
> vide minimal but simple visual rest.

* * * * *

VERMEER (JAN VAN DER MEER VAN DELFT) (1632 - 1675)

*Goldscheider, Ludwig. JAN VERMEER, THE PAINTINGS, Complete Edition.
Translated by R. H. Boothroyd. London: Phaidon Press, Ltd., (c. 1958).
Distributed by Garden City Books, New York. 155 pp. Illus. (34 color
plates, 83 monochrome). Bibliography.

> Sensitive account of Vermeer's use of broad daylight to show how
> light and objects encounter one another and how they become
> spatially visible. Vermeer's palette is analyzed, as well as the
> kinds of usually unnoticed visual textures that have such profound
> effects upon viewers and which Vermeer was able to record magically
> in his paintings. Plates are lovely.

* * * * *

VERONESE, PAOLO (c. 1528 - 1588)

See: COLOR: IDEOLOGY. Berenson, Bernhard. ITALIAN PAINTERS OF THE
RENAISSANCE.

* * * * *

VLAMINCK, MAURICE DE (1876 - 1958)

*Selz, Jean. VLAMINCK. Translated by Graham Snell. The Q.L.P. Art

Series. New York: Corwn Publishers, Inc., n.d. 94 pp. Color and black and white illus. Bibliography.

> Interesting psychological development of Vlaminck's color from deep, dark insecure to a state representing being at peace with himself and his more "joyful color" period. Selz traces Vlaminck's involvement with the Fauves, his influence by Van Gogh, the development of his color ideas mixing subtle tones with pure color, and the use of "juxtaposition." Exceedingly good book for painters - rather than those interested in abstract concepts of color.

* * * * *

VUILLARD, EDOUARD   (1868 - 1940)

*Roger-Marx, Claude. VUILLARD, HIS LIFE AND WORK. New York: Editions de la Maison Francaise, (c. 1946). 211 pp. Mostly black and white illus. Bibliography. Paperbound.

> The color in Vuillard's paintings, filled with mysterious, softly glowing interior light, illuminating the secret faces and surroundings, is described warmly by Roger-Marx. Vuillard's theories are to be discovered and absorbed as are the metaphors of poetry, rather than concretely comprehended.

Russell, John. VUILLARD. Greenwich, Conn.: New York Graphic Society, Ltd., (c. 1971). 238 pp. 17 color, 207 black and white illus., photos. Reading list.

> Information regarding the technique of Vuillard's painting on cardboard and "a la colle," painting with glue as discussed by Jacques Solomon, is particularly informative to the color student. Comments and reminiscences by other contributors fill in impressions without precisely giving information.

* * * * *

WHISTLER, JAMES ABBOTT MCNEILL   (1834 - 1903)

Cary, Elisabeth Luther. THE WORKS OF JAMES MCNEILL WHISTLER. New York: Moffat, Yard and Co., 1913, (c. 1907). 302 pp. Black and white illus. Tentative list of the artist's works.

> Elisabeth Cary relates the technique and color in the paintings of Whistler as the basis for his color theories. She does not exclude Whistler's unique individuality, yet understands and writes of the influences by his peers, environment, and education upon his work and ideas.

Pennell, Elizabeth (Robins) and Joseph. THE WHISTLER JOURNAL. Philadelphia: J. B. Lippincott Co., 1921. xxi, 339 pp. Black and white illus. us.

A biography in journal form as though told by Whistler. Anecdotes reveal the source of his concepts, and his love of light and color. Pleasant, but hardly brilliant.

Chapter 5

COLOR: DECORATION

Chapter 5

COLOR: DECORATION

Anderson, A. Marie. SYLLABUS OF DESIGN AND COLOR. New York,
Milwaukee, Chicago: The Bruce Publishing Co., (c. 1933). viii, 108 pp.
Bibliography.

> Marie Anderson's book is directed towards decoration and cos-
> tume design, and as such is severely dated in principles of
> do's and don'ts.

Birren, Faber. LIGHT, COLOR AND ENVIRONMENT. New York, Cincinnati, Toronto, London, Melbourne: Van Nostrand Reinhold Co., (c. 1969).
131 pp. Color and black and white illus. Bibliography.

> A "Birren" book on how to use color and light to achieve health
> and happiness in any environment. It affords a thorough pre-
> sentation of facts on the biological and psychological effects of
> color - plus historical data and detailed recommendations for the
> resultful use of color in modern human environments.

Bond, Fred. COLOR, HOW TO SEE AND USE IT. A PRACTICAL APPROACH
TO COLOR. "An Exposition of Color Relationships, Basic Procedures in Solv-
ing Color Problems especially Applicable to the Everyday Needs of Color
Photographers, Art Teachers, Art Students, Industrial Designers, Graphic Artists,
Homemakers." San Francisco: Camera Craft Publishing Co., (c. 1954). 167
pp. Color and black and white illus., diagrams, photos, hue selector-mask.

> Fred Bond provides us with the answers to all color problems.
> Basically, it is a simple book written for simple people and
> smacks of 1950's commercialism.

Burris-Meyer, Elizabeth. COLOR AND DESIGN IN THE DECORATIVE ARTS.
New York: Prentice-Hall, Inc., 1940, (c. 1935). xx, 572 pp. Black and
white illus., photos. Bibliography.

> Noble effort overly influenced by style, for Elizabeth Burris-Meyer
> falters in her ability to relate abstract concepts, optical and physi-
> cal theories of color to practical concepts needed by artists and
> designers in today's technological society. She relates color to
> psychological needs of cleanliness, durability, and other contem-

porary image demands.

_____ HISTORICAL COLOR GUIDE: PRIMITIVE TO MODERN TIMES.
(With Thirty Plates in Color). New York: William Helburn, Inc., (c. 1938).
x, 30 pp.

Color schemes represented by size, shape, and physical propor-
tion. Color notes for each period are included that vary in
purpose and intent with the author's personal interests. Strange
concept.

Cheskin, Louis. COLOR FOR PROFIT. New York: Liveright Publishing
Corp., (c. 1951). 164 pp. Illus. (part color).

Parameters defined for the practical colorist whose purpose is
to achieve a definite, immediate goal with its specific gestalt
determined by the marketing expert.

Ketcham, Howard. COLOR PLANNING FOR BUSINESS AND INDUSTRY.
New York: Harper & Brothers, (c. 1958). xiv, 274 pp. Color illus.

An accumulation of information on color application for the
home, office, or industry based upon surveys of individual likes
and dislikes. It is, as Ketchum suggests in his preface, not
based upon theory or any systematic, logical thought, but rather
on what has proven to be successful from his point of view.

Pevsner, Nikolaus. See: COLOR: ARCHITECTURE. PEVSNER. STUDIES IN
ART, ARCHITECTURE AND DESIGN.

*Read, [Sir] Herbert [Edward]. ART AND INDUSTRY AND THE PRINCIPLES OF
INDUSTRIAL DESIGN. Bloomington: Indiana University Press, (c. 1953, 1961).
xvi, 239 pp. Black and white illus. Paperbound.

Herbert Read relates color to man's psychological necessity for
ornamentation. He discusses color as being originally fortuitous
(of the material rather than applied), and generally as a property of pigment or other material. Although he does not include
visual textures as part of color attributes, he discusses the importance of visual textures as an aesthetic.

Walch, Margaret. AMERICAN FABRICS COLOR SOURCE BOOK. New York:
Doric Publishing Co., 1971. 48 boxed folders. Edition limited to 500 copies.

An interesting gestalt approach to choosing and presenting significant color palettes from all civilizations of the world, from prehis-
toric to contemporary man. Visual impression rather than chemical analysis or technical description is the key to the author's
point of view.

Chapter 6

COLOR: DESIGN

Chapter 6

COLOR: DESIGN

Pevsner, Nikolaus. See: COLOR: ARCHITECTURE. PEVSNER, NIKOLAUS. STUDIES IN ART, ARCHITECTURE AND DESIGN.

See also: COLOR: EDUCATION and COLOR: IDEOLOGY.

Chapter 7

COLOR: DISCRIMINATION

Chapter 7

COLOR: DISCRIMINATION

Hering, Ewald. See: COLOR: THEORIES. HERING, EWALD. OUTLINES OF A THEORY OF THE LIGHT SENSE.

Le Grand, Yves. See: COLOR: VISION. Le GRAND, YVES. LIGHT, COLOUR AND VISION.

Trevor-Roper, Patrick THE WORLD THROUGH BLUNTED SIGHT: AN INQUIRY INTO THE INFLUENCE OF DEFECTIVE VISION ON ART AND CHARACTER. Indianapolis, New York: The Bobbs-Merrill Co., Inc., (c. 1970). 191 pp. 29 color plates, 78 in monochrome and 5 line drawings. Bibliography.

> An explanation of altered vision and its implications in the work of various artists. Deals with direct optical phenomena (problems) but with limited significance. Generally disappointing after a fascinating beginning.

Wright, William David. RESEARCHES ON NORMAL AND DEFECTIVE COLOUR VISION. London: Henry Kimpton, 1946. xvi, 383 pp. 233 illus. (part color), charts, graphs, diagrams.

> Important for understanding how we see and why we see color as color. Includes description of the colorimeter designed by the author and used for his experiments on luminosity, color measurement, color mixture, and physiological implications. While primarily a record of experimental data, the book is interesting because of the author's theoretical discussions and his speculations regarding color vision. Technical.

Chapter 8

COLOR: EASEL PAINTING

Chapter 8

COLOR: EASEL PAINTING

Baxandall, Michael. PAINTING AND EXPERIENCE IN FIFTEENTH CENTURY ITALY: A/PRIMER IN THE SOCIAL HISTORY OF PICTORIAL STYLE. London: Oxford University Press, (c. 1972). 165 pp. Illus. (part color).

> Michael Baxandall takes a social-historical approach to the visual development and habits of the painters. His argument that the artist is a product of his environment is not a new one, but his insights and particular arguments are winsome. Color theory approached from such a point of view is somewhat novel.

Berckelaers, Ferdinand Louis. DICTIONARY OF ABSTRACT PAINTING. Translated by Lionel Izod, et al. New York: Tudor Publishing Co., 1957. 304 pp. Illus. (part color). Bibliography.

> A good introductory reference to those artists whose ideas of color had great relevance in the abstract movement. The history is short but nicely documented.

Birren, Faber. HISTORY OF COLOR IN PAINTING; WITH NEW PRINCIPLES OF COLOR EXPRESSION. New York: Reinhold Publishing Corp., (c. 1965). 372 pp. Illus., color plates. Bibliography.

> An excellent introduction for the beginning color student to the various areas of study he may follow. The book includes many optical theories; it approaches color ideas through the palettes and techniques of artists, and relates them to their personalities. Faber Birren discusses concepts of color harmonies and introduces the reader to the psychology of color and color expression, as well as to the principles of perception.

Churchill, Winston. PAINTING AS A PASTIME. New York: Cornerstone Library Publications. Reprinted 1965. vi, 32 pp. 18 color plates. (Hardcover edition was published in the United States in 1950 by the McGraw-Hill Book Co., Inc. The essay "Painting as a Pastime" is reprinted from Sir Winston Churchill's book AMID THESE STORMS [c. 1932] by permission of the publishers, Charles Scribner's Sons, N.Y.)

Winston Churchill as a sensitive observer of nature and amateur painter brings freshness to perception of light and color.

THE FUNCTIONS OF COLOR IN PAINTING. Washington: Philips Memorial Gallery, 1941. 50 pp. An educational loan exhibition.

The catalog of the functions of color in painting is an amazing document that categorizes widely divergent color concepts in a concise and readable form. The writing reflects a nineteenth-century attitude about twentieth-century painters but is highly enjoyable.

Goldwater, Robert, and Treves, Marco, eds. ARTISTS ON ART, FROM THE XIV TO THE XX CENTURY. 3rd ed. New York: Pantheon Books, Inc., 1958, (c. 1945). xii, 499 pp. 100 black and white illus.

As the artists speak on art, each touches upon his color concept: Alberti felt arbitrary color contrasts meant harmony; Homer discusses the vitues of direct out-of-door light and reflected light, which include the blending and suffusing of several luminations; Ingres discusses Rubens and Van Dyck as representing "bad schools of color."

Guptill, Arthur L. COLOR IN SKETCHING AND RENDERING. Introduction by J. Floyd Yewell. New York: Reinhold Publishing Corp., (1935). xxiv, 348 pp. Mostly color illus.

A way of comprehending color by doing, and through doing, seeing. Helpful for the painting student, particularly those who need help in getting started with their craft. The suggestions concerning color harmony, or altering and correcting color, may provide the student with security, but it is doubtful if his imagination will be stimulated.

*Haftmann, Werner. PAINTING IN THE TWENTIETH CENTURY. Translated by R. Manheim. New York: Frederick A. Praeger, Inc., 1960. (Completely revised version of the German editions published in 1954-55 and 1957 by Prestel Verlag, Munich.) Vol. 1 - 430 pp. Vol. 2 - 539 pp. Mostly black and white illus.

Werner Haftmann approaches art of the twentieth century with an appropriate owareness of the role of color and form to the meaning of painting. Therefore, he develops quite brilliantly the color theories of each of the artists he includes, i.e., Cezanne, Matisse, Klee, Kandinsky, Rousseau, de Chirico, Miro, Picasso, and the ideas of schools of painters, i.e., the Impressionists, the Nabis, Futurists, Orphism, Fauves, Magic Realists, and Expressionists.

Haines, F. Merlin. TONE AND COLOUR IN LANDSCAPE PAINTING; A SIMPLE EXPLANATION OF THE PRINCIPLES DECIDING THE APPARENT TONES AND COLOURS OF OBJECTS IN THE OPEN AIR. Forword by Stephen Bone.

London: Adam & Charles Black, (1954).   ix, 93 pp.   Frontispiece in color
and 22 diagrams.

> Merlin Haines discusses nature and provides suggestions for
> translating natural phenomena to the two-dimentional surface.
> While interesting reading, it is a book that would be of great-
> er interest to the Sunday painter than to the serious student
> of color.

*Hawthorne, Mrs. Charles W.   HAWTHORNE ON PAINTING.   Introduction
by Edwin Dickinson, appreciation by Hans Hofmann, from student's notes col-
lected by Mrs. Charles W. Hawthorne.   New York: Dover Publications, Inc.,
(c. 1938, 1960).   (Enlarged republication of the work published by the Pitman
Publishing Corp. in 1938.) xiv, 91 pp.

> Hawthorne's visual acuity and perception of color in nature is
> unique and the source of endless stimulation to the development
> of the role of color in his teaching.

Henri, Robert.   THE ART SPIRIT; NOTES, ARTICLES, FRAGMENTS OF LETTERS
AND TALKS TO STUDENTS, BEARING ON THE CONCEPT AND TECHNIQUE
OF PICTURE MAKING, THE STUDY OF ART GENERALLY, AND ON APPRE-
CIATION.   Compiled by Margery Ryerson, a New Issue with an Introduction
by Forbes Watson.   Philadelphia and London: J. B. Lippincott Co., (c. 1923,
1930).   x, 292 pp.   16 black and white illus.

> THE ART SPIRIT embodies the entire system of Henri's teaching.
> His color ideas are perceptual in origin and free in spirit.

Knobler, Nathan.   THE VISUAL DIALOGUE; AN INTRODUCTION TO THE AP-
PRECIATION OF ART.   New York, Chicago, San Francisco, Toronto, London:
Holt, Rinehart and Winston, Inc., n.d. x, 342 pp.   Black and white and
color illus., photos.   Bibliography.

> Knobler discusses a variety of concepts: color as a space indicator;
> color related to the two-dimensional surface; local color; the color-
> solid; and, color as paint.   The separate chapter on color theory
> deals with optics, value, and saturation, but is of less interest than
> the color ideas posed throughout the book.

Lamb, Lynton.   PREPARATION FOR PAINTING; THE PURPOSE AND MATERIALS
OF THE ARTIST.   Baltimore: Penguin Books, Inc., 1960.   (First published by
the Oxford University Press, 1954).   xv, 175 pp.   Black and white illus. Paperbound.

> Lynton Lamb feels that the artist need only know about mixing
> paint; once this knowledge is acquired, the artist can express and
> represent color sensations.   He does suggest, However, that the
> mixture of pigment be an interpretation of light.   Although his
> concept is simple, he reflects the general attitudes of his day,
> as well as those still taught in many schools.

Lowry, Bates.   THE VISUAL EXPERIENCE; AN INTRODUCTION TO ART.   Engle-

wood Cliffs, N. J.: Prentice-Hall, Inc.; New York: Harry N. Abrams, Inc.,
n.d. 272 pp. Color and black and white illus.

> Dark and light contrast, and middle steps of grey related to the
> basic phenomena of simultaneous contrast, form a major part of
> Bates Lowry's color theory. His theories of chromatic color re-
> late to the principle of closure, and he applied these ideas to
> his analysis of paintings.

*Merrifield, Mary P. ORIGINAL TREATISES ON THE ARTS OF PAINTING. With
a new introduction and glossary by S. M. Alexander. 2 vols. New York: Dover
Publications, (c. 1967). ix, 918 pp.

> A more personal and poetic account of methods and materials in
> the art of painting from the original writings of the masters. Effects
> of color and light are described related to the techniques of the time.
> An aesthetic is implied and related to achieving realistic results. This
> point of view is not unlike Eastlake's writing of approximately the
> same time.

Moreau-Vauthier, Charles. THE TECHNIQUE OF PAINTING. Preface by Etienne
Dinet. London: W. Heinemann, 1912; New York: G. P. Putnam's Sons, (c. 1928).
xvi, 260 pp. Color frontispiece, 24 plates (8 in color).

> A concept of color is inferred by its relationship to a specific tech-
> nique in painting. The primary purpose of the book is to tell how to
> achieve certain colors and color effects. There are many valuable
> quotations by scientists and artists.

Protter, Eric, ed. PAINTERS ON PAINTING. New York: Grosset & Dunlap. Inc.,
(c. 1963). xvi, 272 pp. Black and white illus. Bibliography. Paperbound.

> A lovely selection of thoughts by painters primarily concerning
> painting but always dealing with a unique point of view on color.

Read, Sir Herbert Edward. A CONCISE HISTORY OF MODERN PAINTING. New
York: Praeger, (1959). 376 pp. Illus. (part color). "Text references."
Bibliography.

> Although one of Read's lesser books, it traces concepts of color
> through the modern movements in a concise and informative way.

_____. THE PHILOSOPHY OF MODERN ART. New York: Meridian Books,
1955, (c. 1952). (Reprinted by arrangement with Horizon Press, Inc.) x, 309 pp.
Paperbound.

> The essay on Gauguin is rich in color insight. Herbert Read develops
> his theory of Gauguin's color by analyzing the paintings as well as
> Gauguin's verbal statements concerning his intentions in art.

Taylor, John F. A. DESIGN AND EXPRESSION IN THE VISUAL ARTS. New York:

Dover Publications, Inc., (c. 1964). x, 245 pp. Mostly black and white illus.
Elevations. Paperbound.

> John Taylor approaches color as one of those elements in
> our lives that cannot be defined, only exhibited. He defines
> physical light and sensed light, describing color as a sub-
> jective response. He compares and analyzes the color seen
> by the discriminating, painterly eye, to color perceived by
> the less discriminating eye. He has a separate vocabulary to
> define what the eye sees.

*Venturi, Lionello. PAINTING AND PAINTERS; HOW TO LOOK AT A PIC-
TURE FROM GIOTTO TO CHAGALL. New York: Charles Scribner's Sons,
1945. xx, 250 pp. Black and white illus.

> Lionello Venturi was concerned with the entire meaning of a
> work of art. He recognized the need for unity of subject
> matter, content, as well as the "physical elements" of form,
> line, plasticity, and color. His color analysis is based upon
> concepts related to physical matters and painterly techniques,
> such as chiaroscuro, contours, light and shodow. His ideas
> are penetrating and poetic.

*Waddington, C. H. BEHIND APPEARANCE: A STUDY OF THE RELATIONS
BETWEEN PAINTING AND THE NATURAL SCIENCES IN THIS CENTURY.
Cambridge: The M.I.T. Press., (c. 1969, 1970). x, 256 pp. Color and
black and white illus.

> C. H. Waddington examines the way artists and scientists view the
> material world in the twentieth-century. She has particular interest
> in the opposing point of view between rationalists and mystics, and
> the validity of each stand. The book is important as a supplementary
> study to anytone building color concepts or theories.

Chapter 9

COLOR: EDUCATION

Chapter 9

COLOR: EDUCATION

*Albers, Josef. INTERACTION OF COLOR. 2 vols. New Haven and London: Yale University Press, (c. 1963). Vol. 1 - 80 pp. Text with black and white illus. Vol. 2 - 80 folders (color plates) with commentary.

> INTERACTION OF COLOR is a fascinating visual statement. Albers' color concepts are based upon the discoveries of Chevreul, Bezold, and Weber-Fechner. As an artist, his method of relating those theories to his own work differs in the sense that they are not used as tools for teaching. The book is a valuable perceptual and optical document of a process, even though it tends to be regarded as dogma. The plates are technically superb and seductive.

*Bayer, Herbert; Gropius, Walter; and Gropius, Ise, eds. BAUHAUS. 1919-1928. New York: The Museum of Modern Art, (c. 1938). 224 pp. Black and white illus. Bibliography.

> BAUHAUS brings together course outlines and broad concepts basic to the teaching as well as hundreds of faculty and student photographs. Information includes abstract and scientific color theories related to the pragmatic, such as how to paint on walls, to use color in space, to create stain glass, to paint on canvas, or to use color in weaving.

Birren, Faber. COLOR, A SURVEY IN WORDS AND PICTURES, FROM ANCIENT MYSTICISM TO MODERN SCIENCE. New Hyde Park, N. Y.: University Books, Inc., (c. 1963). 223 pp. Mostly black and white illus., diagrams.

> Although a fascinating collection of color information related to magic, religion or general color theories, and their impact upon society, it is written in a journalistic, uninspired way. Unfortunately, much of the material has been taken out of context and is bewildering.

_____ FUNCTIONAL COLOR, A BOOK OF FACTS AND RESEARCH, MEANT TO INSPIRE MORE RATIONAL METHODS IN THE SOLUTION OF COLOR PROBLEMS. New York: The Crimson Press, 1937. 124 pp. Illus. (part color). Bibliography.

Birren's potpourri of color is approached through a scramble of color modes and attributes attached to physical and sometimes psychological needs.

*Burnham, Robert W., et al. COLOR, A GUIDE TO BASIC FACTS AND CONCEPTS. "A report of the Inter-Society Color Council Subcommittee for Problem 20: Basic Elements of Color Education." New York, London, Sydney: John Wiley & Sons, Inc., (c. 1963). xi, 249 pp. Illus. (part color), diagrmas. Bibliography.

A study to ascertain the basic principles which should be included in any elementary teaching of color. Includes a definition of color and its attributes as a visual experience, applied facts dealing with color measurements, marginal facts concerning color-vision theory, assessment of color aptitudes, and experimental color aesthetics.

*Church, Arthur Herbert. COLOUR: AN ELEMENTARY MANUAL FOR STUDENTS. London, Paris, New York, Melbourne: Cassell and Co., Ltd., 1887. viii, 192 six-colored plates. Black and white illus., diagrams.

Arthur Church bases his teachings upon the research carried out by Chevreul, Maxwell, Helmholtz, W. Benson, and W. Von Bezold. Excellent resource book. Discusses the uses and modifications of pigment mixtures.

Dickson, T. Elder. AN INTRODUCTION TO COLOUR. London: Sir Isaac Pitman & Sons, Ltd., 1932. viii, 68 pp. Color and black and white illus.

This book includes presentation of the scientific background of color to develop experiments for class work, including perception of simultaneous contrast. Dickson introduces ideas to develop color harmonies.

*Evans, Ralph Merril. AN INTRODUCTION TO COLOR. New York: John Wiley & Sons, Inc. London: Chapman & Hall, Ltd., 1948. x, 340 pp. 15 color plates. Black and white illus., diagrams, charts, graphs. Bibliography.

A very good basic book for the teacher or art student. Ralph Evans' book contains information about light, perception, color vision, color measurement, specification of color, optical phenomena, colorants, paints, and pigments. His ideas of color harmony are based upon Pope's and do not occupy too many pages. (See page 127.)

*Graves, Maitland. COLOR FUNDAMENTALS; WITH 100 COLOR SCHEMES. New York, Toronto, London: McGraw-Hill Book Co., Inc., (c. 1952). xi, 206 pp. Color and black and white illus. Diagrams.

Maitland Graves introduces light and color concepts, color and colorant concepts, ways to measure colors, perception of additive and subtractive mixes in light experiments, and describes effects of illuminants on colorants and colorant mixtures.

He deals with color sensation and its modifiers, and finally
with the Munsell system and the psychological specifications
of colorants within it. Important reading but loses direction.

_____. THE ART OF COLOR AND DESIGN. 2nd ed. New York: Mc-
Graw-Hill Book Co., 1951. xvi, 439 pp. Mostly black and white illus.,
photos. Glossary.

A highly structured analysis of the elements to be considered
in the study of color and design. The thinking reflects the
strong visual sense of order developed by the Bauhaus. However, the influence of the verbalization of visual rules in this
way subordinates visual curiosity and learning to a secondary
role in the learning process. The basic information is useful
for beginning teachers - includes concepts of color harmony,
color cards, color schemes, color characteristics, color contrasts, color sensations, principles of design, and color nota-
tions based upon Munsell.

*Itten, Johannes. DESIGN AND FORM: THE BASIC COURSE AT THE BAU-
HAUS. Translated by John Maass. New York: Reinhold Publishing Corp.,
(c. 1964). 190 pp. Black and white illus., photos, diagrams.

In Johannes Itten's book, color theory is examined primarily
through the use of pigment, rather than as phenomena. Color
is considered as paint and part of a sensuous and spiritual
system of expression. Physical textures are discussed as visual
phenomena, but not as part of a color and light theory. It is
a charming book for the student, teacher, or artist.

* _____. THE ART OF COLOR: THE SUBJECTIVE EXPERIENCE AND OBJEC-
TIVE RATIONALE OF COLOR. Translated by Ernst van Haagen. New York: Reinhold Publishing Corp., (c. 1961). 155 pp. Mostly color illus., photos, diagrams.

Classical book by Itten, summarizing his ideas developed while
a teacher at the Bauhaus. Psychologically his color concepts
were and are inclined toward subjectivity. His theories are
based upon Newton and Chevreul. Itten's personal contribution is in the area of his "concord of colors" and "subjective
timbre." His seven-color contrast principle is confusing, as
simultaneous contrast is listed separately rather than as the
principal change encompassing all other contrast changes.

_____. THE ELEMENTS OF COLOR; A TREATISE ON THE COLOR SYSTEM
OF JOHANNES ITTEN, BASED ON HIS BOOK THE ART OF COLOR. Edited
by Faber Birren, translated by Ernst Van Haagen. New York, Cincinnati,
Toronto, London, Melbourne: Van Nostrand Reinhold Co., (c. 1970). 96 pp.
Mostly color illus. Diagrams.

A simplification and condensation of THE ART OF COLOR.

Jacobs, Michael. THE ART OF COLOUR. Garden City, N.Y.: Doubleday, Page & Co., 1923. xiv, 90 pp. Color illus., charts.

> Michael Jacobs' system for teaching the art of color is based upon the color theories of Helmholtz and Tyndall. He shifts from Newtonian primaries to spectral primaries and proceeds to equate the latter with pigment (oil paint) names. Concepts of color harmonies die hard, and it is interesting to compare the same ideas presented today. Finally, he applies technology and color psychology to practical uses for the printer, weaver, costume designer, and even flower arranger. Contains a useful dictionary of colors with chemical names and identification in the spectrum.

Kallop, Edward, ed. THE LOGIC AND MAGIC OF COLOR. New York: The Cooper Union Museum., (c. 1960). 36 pp. Introduction. Bibliography.

> This book derives from an exhibition celebrating the centennial anniversary of the Cooper Union. History of color dealing in a simple concise way with optics, chemistry, systems of measurements, and the psychology of color. It also has its own useful bibliography.

*Maycock, Mark M. A CLASS-BOOK OF COLOR; INCLUDING COLOR DEFINITIONS, COLOR SCALING, AND THE HARMONY OF COLORS. Springfield, Mass.: Milton Bradley Co., (c. 1895). 63 pp. Color and black and white illus., diagrams.

> A book of excercises designed for the inexperienced teacher dealing with very young children. Charming comparisons of color in pigment to color in nature and simple dogma of harmonies, also descriptions of effects of simultaneous contrast.

*Rood, Ogden N. STUDENT'S TEXT-BOOK OF COLOR; OR MODERN CHROMATICS WITH APPLICATIONS TO ART AND INDUSTRY. New York: D. Appleton and Co., 1908. viii, 329 pp. 130 original black and white illus.

> Rood's excellent study of color is based upon the optical theories and principles of Thomas Young as modified by Helmholtz and Maxwell. Rood's contribution to art education is valuable as he discarded the concept of harmonies and "musical theories." He provides solid information for the artist.

Sargent, Walter. THE ENJOYMENT AND USE OF COLOR. New York: Charles Scribner's Sons, 1924, (c. 1923). xi, 274 pp. Color and black and white illus., diagrams.

> Deals with color as sensation, attributes of hue, value and intensity, optical phenomena, concepts of color harmony, and color perceived in nature. Excellent balance between art and science.

Sloan, John. GIST OF ART, By John Sloan; PRINCIPLES AND PRACTICE EXPOUNDED IN THE CLASSROOM AND STUDIO, RECORDED WITH THE ASSISTANCE OF HELEN FARR. New York: American Artist's Group, Inc., (c. 1939). Black and white illus., diagrams.

> Not surprisingly, John Sloan includes diagrams for color-textures, progressions, color triangles, and arrangement of the palette. He gives the names of "right" pigment colors and color chords to illustrate his color theories. His subjective concepts include strong feelings about the power of color, i.e., advancing and receding colors as well as warm and cool colors. Fascinating, not unlike one of his paintings, but a curiosity.

Sloane, Patricia. COLOUR: BASIC PRINCIPLES NEW DIRECTIONS. New York: Reinhold Book Corp., n.d. Mostly black and white illus., diagrams. Bibliography. Paperbound.

> Although Patricia Sloane writes broadly with references to excellent sources in optics and in art, the underlying assumption is that the importance of color relates to individual taste. Interesting bibliography.

*Vanderpoel, Emily Noyes. COLOR PROBLEMS; A PRACTICAL MANUAL FOR THE LAY STUDENT OF COLOR. New York, London, and Bombay: Longmans, Green, and Co., 1903. xv, 137 pp.. 117 color plates. Bibliography.

> The relation of color and light to music and sound and color qualities perceived in nature provide the structure upon which Emily Vanderpoel builds her color theories. She examines problems of the human eye, and the theories of Chevruel, Ogden Rood, and other scientists.

Chapter 10

COLOR: FORM

Chapter 10

COLOR: FORM

Clark, Kenneth. THE NUDE; A STUDY IN IDEAL FORM. The A. W. Mellon Lectures in the Fine Arts 1953, National Gallery of Art, Washington, Bollingen Series, vol. 35, no. 2. New York: Pantheon Books, Inc., (c. 1956). xxi, 458 pp. 298 black and white illus. Paperbound.

> Although Kenneth Clark's forte of appreciation and psychological interpretation is in form, he is aware of the force of light and color in the history of the art of the nude. He writes gracefully of the role of light and color upon the form of the nude in its changing historical context.

Herbert, Robert L. THE ART CRITICISM OF JOHN RUSKIN. Garden City, N.Y.: Doubleday & Co. Inc. (Anchor Books), (c. 1964). xliii, 430 pp. Paperbound.

> John Ruskin discusses color perceived by the artist as optimum when he can approach as nearly as possible the condition of infantine sight. His writing about color is as maddening as his other ideas, for he combines genius of perception with irresponsibility – for example, how to achieve infantine color sight.

Minnaert, M. THE NATURE OF LIGHT AND COLOR IN THE OPEN AIR. Translated by H. M. Kremer-Priest, revised by K. E. Bryan Jay. New York Dover Publications, Inc., 1954. viii, 362 pp. Black and white illus., diagrams. Paperbound.

> Fascinating record by a naturalist and scientist of optical phenomena observed in nature and explained mathematically and scientifically. However, the author has genuine concern for sensory perception and learning. The book contains much information about such phenomena as rainbows, haloes, and coronae as well as intensity and brightness of light and after-images. His perceptual observations, which make his book of interest to the artist, include concepts of light and color of the sky and in the landscape.

Stokes, Adrian. STONES OF RIMINI. New York: Schocken Books, (1969). 263 pp. 48 black and white illus. Paperbound.

> Adrian Stokes' basic theme is that understanding the visual arts necessitates cherishing some fantasy of the material that stimulated the

artist. Light and color emerge as strong elements in the creation of the visual fantasy. Reality, as materials, is designed to reflect light, absorb sun, and become other modes of appearance. Beautiful book.

Chapter 11

COLOR: IMAGERY

Chapter 11

COLOR: IMAGERY

Carraher, Ronald G., and Thurston, Jacqueline B. OPTICAL ILLUSIONS AND THE VISUAL ARTS. New York, London: Reinhold Publishing Corp., (c. 1966). 127 pp. Black and white illus.

> Basic book for understanding such optical effects as complementary color systems or after-images, brightness, contrast, irradiation, principles of closure, and figure ground relationships.

*Stokes, Adrian. COLOUR AND FORM. London: Faber & Faber, Ltd., (1937). 135 pp.

> An aesthetic study of the perception of form based upon recognition of total color configuration. The author's scientific training, philosophical and mystical leanings, and love of painting are constantly evident. He says, "Color properly conceived is a principle of creation."

Whyte, Lancelot Law, ed. ASPECTS OF FORM; A SYMPOSIUM ON FORM IN NATURE AND ART. Preface by Herbert Read. Bloomington: Indiana University Press, (c. 1951). 249 pp. Black and white illus. Introduction. Chronological survey on form. Bibliography. Paperbound.

> Among the different points of view presented at the symposium is Cott's fascinating information describing difficulty in perceiving natural form because of colored patterns, which obliterate form or contour. He describes color camouflage, as well as warning coloration, color allurement, and raises problems of color conflict.

> Lorenz's and Arnheim's essays contain important color perception information. Gombrich deals with abstraction of color as part of the process of a symbolic substitution in art.

Chapter 12

COLOR: HARMONY

Chapter 12

COLOR: HARMONY

Abbott, Arthur B. THE COLOR OF LIFE. New York, London: McGraw-Hill Book Co. Inc., 1947. xxi, 294 pp. 7 color plates. Bibliography.

> An anthology of color information touching breezily upon color and light, color and color chemistry in nature, color as manufactured by man, and color harmonies, all of which are based upon Faber Birren's color wheel.

Ellinger, Richard G. COLOR STRUCTURE AND DESIGN. Scranton, Pa.: International Textbook Company, (c. 1963). xii, 144 pp. Illus. (part color).

> An elementary reader for basic concepts of color organization.

Koblo, Martin. WORLD OF COLOR; AN INTRODUCTION TO THE THEORY AND USE OF COLOR IN ART. Translated by Ian F. Finlay. New York: McGraw-Hill Book Co., (c. 1963). Illus. (part color).

> A most elementary color theory intended for the artist who is interested in the subjective, expressionistic qualities of color. He structures arbitrary yet interesting relationships such as the ideas of Ostwald and the perceived phenomena of Goethe or the world of light contrasted to the technical matters of pigment and media.

McDonald, Sterling B. COLOR HARMONY, WITH THE MCDONALD CALIBRATOR. Chicago, New York, Toronto, Mexico City: Wilcox & Follett Co., (c. 1949). 123 pp. Color and black and white illus. Bibliography.

> The Sterling McDonald physical calibrator becomes the authority for allowing colors to be used together to create color harmony. A bizarre idea with little relation to complex visual phenomena.

Renner, Paul. COLOR: ORDER AND HARMONY; A COLOR THEORY FOR ARTISTS AND CRAFTSMEN. Translated by Alexander Nesbitt. New York: Reinhold Publishing Corp., (c. 1964). 80 pp. Color and black and white illus.

> Pleasant basic book covering color as pigment, problems of color perception, color and the natural sciences, and a variety of concepts related to color harmony.

Chapter 13

COLORIMETRY

Chapter 13

COLORIMETRY

American Society for Testing Materials and The Inter-Society Color Council. SYMPOSIUM ON COLOR-ITS SPECIFICATION AND USE IN EVALUATING THE APPEARANCE OF MATERIALS. Philadelphia: American Society for Testing Materials, 1941. iii, 79 pp. Black and white illus., tables, graphs. Bibliography.

> Papers based upon the 1941 symposium on color, color specification, and use in evaluating the appearance of material. The introduction to color by Deane B. Judd is excellent.

Hardy, Arthur C. HANDBOOK OF COLORIMETRY. Prepared by the Staff of the Color Measurement Laboratory, Massachusetts Institute of Technology. Cambridge, Mass.: The M.I.T. Press, 1936. v, 87 pp. Graphs, tables, charts.

> HANDBOOK OF COLORIMENTRY is based upon the physical basis of color specification. The book supplies graphs and charts which facilitate this specification.

Judd, Deane B., and Wyszecki, Gunter. See: COLOR: VISION. Judd, Deane B., and Wyszecki, Gunter. COLOR IN BUSINESS, SCIENCE, AND INDUSTRY.

*Optical Society of America. Committee on Colorimetry. THE SCIENCE OF COLOR. New York: Thomas Y. Crowell Co., (1953). xiii, 385 pp. Black and white illus., tables, photos, 25 color plates.

> Outstanding and authoritative compilation of material in the field of colorimetrics. Particularly useful for its clear terminology and summary of available physical, psychophysical, and psychological data relating color to its stimulus conditions. Excellent source book for developing a sense of logic in thinking about color problems. References include works of Helmholtz, Boring, Purkinje, Bezold, Hering, Maxwell, Katz, Gibson, Judd, Fechner, and Fresnel besides other classical referents.

Wright, William David. THE MEASUREMENT OF COLOR. 4th ed. New York, Cincinnati, Toronto, London, Melbourne: Van Nostrand Reinhold Co., (c. 1969). x, 340 pp. Some color illus., graphs, diagrams, tables.

Primarily valuable for its explanation of the trichromatic system of color measurement, which is the fundamental measuring system for color specification adopted by the Commission Internationale de l'Eclairage in 1931. Also excellent chapters on perception of light and color, color matching, and color discrimination.

Chapter 14

COLOR: IDEOLOGY

Chapter 14

COLOR: IDEOLOGY

*Agee, William C. SYNCHROMISM AND COLOR PRINCIPLES IN AMERICAN PAINTING, 1910-1930. New York: M. Knoedler & Co., Inc., 1965. 53 pp. Color and black and white illus.

> Excellent historical source for understanding the differences be-
> tween the "Simultanistes" of Robert Delaunay and the "Synchro-
> mists" of Morgan Russell, and tracing the development of the op-
> tical use of color in painting.

Apollinaire, Guillaume. THE CUBIST PAINTERS; AESTHETICS MEDITATIONS 1913. Translated by Lionel Abel. The Documents of Modern Art, vol. 1. New York: George Wittenborn, Inc., 1962. 65 pp. Black and white illus. Bibliography.

> Guillaume Appollinaire's aesthetic meditations include color-
> metaphor notes in his poem to the cubists. Lovely yet harsh.

Ashton, Dore. THE UNKNOWN SHORE, A VIEW OF CONTEMPORARY ART. Boston and Toronto: Little, Brown and Co., (c. 1962). xviii, 265 pp. Black and white illus. Index.

> A color environment is spun out as Miss Ashton weaves her
> magic web of influences, reactions, and interactions among
> painters and their ideas.

*Barnes, Albert C. THE ART IN PAINTING. 3rd ed. Rev., enl. New York: Harcourt, Brace and Co. (c. 1925, 1928, 1937). xx, 522 pp. Black and white illus.

> Most informative in dealing with color in academicism, or color
> as part of form and light, color as part of the Flemish, Florentine,
> Venetian, French, and German tradition in painting, ideas of
> color composition, or color mysticism. Includes thoughts relating
> color to contemporary art based upon Cezanne's theories of light
> and color as observed in his paintings and watercolors.

Battcock, Gregory, ed. MINIMAL ART; A CRITICAL ANTHOLOGY. New

York: E. P. Dutton & Co., Inc., (c. 1968). 448 pp. Black and white illus. Paperbound.

> Most of the authors who deal with the most advanced concepts of art touch upon the role and meaning of color. E. C. Goossen is one who writes most lucidly and at length of the importance of color, beginning with Hegel who identified color in painting as the element that separated painting from its sister arts. "Color" as concept is used differently by each writer: Sharp's "luminism" essay provides good history and excellent reporting of the light scene of the 1950's.

Baur, John I. H. REVOLUTION AND TRADITION IN MODERN AMERICAN ART. New York, Washington, and London: Frederick A. Praeger, Inc., 1967. (The original clothbound edition of this book was published in 1951 by the Harvard University Press, Cambridge, Mass.) xxii, 170 pp. Black and white illus.

> A good basic book covering the habits and contributions of American artists from the Primitives and Realists, through the Impressionists, Romantic Realists, Expressionists, and Abstractionists.

*Berenson, Bernhard. ITALIAN PAINTERS OF THE RENAISSANCE. 2nd impression. London, England: Phaidon Press, Ltd., 1953. Distributed by Garden City Books, New York. xiii, 488 pp. 16 color plates, 400 black and white plates. Index.

> The four essays contained in this volume were first published separately from 1894 to 1907. The present illustrated edition is published by arrangement with Clarendon Press, Oxford, and the Oxford University Press, New York. This volume has been produced in collaboration with the Samuel H. Kress Foundation as a tribute to Bernhard Berenson and in appreciation of more than a quarter-century of friendship and cooperation in the field of Renaissance painting between Bernhard Berenson and Samuel H. Kress.

> Bernhard Berenson's tremendous appreciation for the color of the Venetians is reinforced by his analysis, descriptions, and examples. Color is less important to the Florentines or the Central Italians. He writes of color well although conventionally.

Burnham, Jack. THE STRUCTURE OF ART. New York: George Braziller, Inc., (c. 1971). xii, 195 pp. Black and white illus. Bibliography.

> Color as an element within a mythical structure and color as a means within a conceptual structure are all within the fascinating philosophy of Burnham who establishes the art experience as one dependent upon communication by the organization of specific relationships between artist (art) and viewer. He deals therefore with color as sign or symbol, but strangely avoids any real commitment to meaning, as in his discussion of such artists as Kelly,

Don Judd, or Stella and their color ideas.

Burnham, Robert W., et al. See: COLOR: EDUCATION. Burnham, Robert W., et al. COLOR, A GUIDE TO BASIC FACTS AND CONCEPTS.

Calas, Nicolas and Elena. ICONS AND IMAGES OF THE SIXTIES. New York: E. P. Dutton & Co., Inc., 1971. 347 pp. ·Black and white illus.

> Nicolas and Elena Calas use two forms of inquiry to interpret the contemporary art scene (since abstract expressionism). These are the pragmatic-genetic method and the formalists'. The formalists' approach involves accounting for retinal effects of combinations of colors and forms as in the case of Michael Fried's analysis of Stella. Either method approaches concepts of color as perceived in art in a detailed and highly articulate way.

Clough, Rosa Trillo. FUTURISM: THE STORY OF A MODERN ART MOVE-MENT, A NEW APPRAISAL. New York: Philosophical Library, Inc., (c. 1961). 297 pp. Black and white illus.

> The color concepts of Futurism emerged from the theories of Impressionism and Cubism, and foreshadowed many of the color theories prevalent today among optical, kinetic, and minimal artists. Pure color, or color without reference to human expres-sion or feeling, was part of their goal. Little attention is given to the physiological effect upon the viewer.

Fenollosa, Ernest F. EPOCHS OF CHINESE & JAPANESE ART, AN OUT-LINE HISTORY OF EAST ASIATIC DESIGN. Rev. ed. 2 vols. New York: Dover Publications, Inc. 1963. (Unabridged republication of the second [1913] edition of the work first published by Frederick A. Stokes Co. and William Heinemann in 1912.) xxxvii, 204 pp. Black and white illus., diagrams. Copious notes by Prof. Petrucci. Paperbound.

> In Ernest Fenollosa's classic history of Chinese and Japanese art, color is one of the elements that emerges as an individ-ual and local distinctive force - unlike form which can be visually traced through specific times and localities. Includes such color information as "Notan," dark and light spotting (closest to our chiaroscuro), experiments of Hokusai in color, color as decoration, and ideal color.

Friedlander, Max J. EARLY NETHERLANDISH PAINTING FROM VAN EYCK TO BRUEGEL. Translated by Marguerite Kay, edited with notes by F. Gross-man. London: Phaidon Publishers, Inc., 1956. Distributed by Garden City Books, New York. vii, 425 pp. Color and black and white illus.

> Max Friedlander's descriptions of colors used by each of the Flemish artists is remote, erudite, and informative. He is careful not to develop any theories of his own.

Color: Ideology

* _____. ON ART AND CONNOISSEURSHIP. Translated by Tancred Borenius. Boston: Beacon Press, 1960. (First published in 1942 by Bruno Cassirer, Ltd.) 284 pp. 40 black and white illus. Introduction. Paperbound.

> Form, color, tonality, light, and gold are specific conceptual elements Friedlander deals with in developing his theses of artists striving toward the perfect illusion. He writes as the connoisseur, one who has had a lifetime or involvement with art specifically rather than with psychology or science. His theories of color emerge naturally, from art itself.

Fry, Roger. FRENCH, FLEMISH AND BRITISH ART. New York: Coward-McCann, Inc., 1951. xii, 215 pp. Black and white illus. Index of artists.

> Roger Fry is interested in color and design as they relate to the spiritual atmosphere in paintings. His descriptions of the accepted and applied color theories help in understanding the art of the French, Flemish, and British. He touches upon concepts of "modes of appearances," but it is doubtful and unimportant that these observations are scientifically based.

Gardiner, Henry G., et al. COLOR & FORM, 1909-1914; THE ORIGIN AND EVOLUTION OF ABSTRACT PAINTING IN FUTURISM, ORPHISM, RAYONISM, SYNCHRONISM AND THE BLUE RIDER. San Diego: Fine Arts Gallery of San Diego, (c. 1970). 103 pp. Color and black and white illus. Bibliography.

> An excellent source for the concepts of Futurism, Orphism, Rayonnism, Synchromism, and Blue Rider. Especially fascinating analysis of such people as Robert Delaunay and his unique point of view and interpretation of Chevreul's law of simultaneity.

Golding, John. CUBISM, A HISTORY AND ANALYSIS 1907-1914. New York: George Wittenborn, Inc., (c. 1959). 207 pp. Mostly black and white illus.

> Interesting analysis of the way the Cubists thought of and used color related to their pictorial ideas as well as their respective personal differences. Their contributions included the introduction of physical material as color and physical-visual texture to the two-dimensional surface.

Gray, Camilla. THE RUSSIAN EXPERIMENT IN ART 1863-1922. New York: Harry N. Abrams, Inc., (c. 1962). Distributed by New American Library. 296 pp. Illus. (part color), photos. Bibliography. Paperbound.

> From the beginning, color was an important element in the work of the Russian artist. It was used as metaphor, as its own reality, as a decorative and seductive tool. The author follows color concepts as another thread in the rich tapestry of art conceived

of as spiritual reality to propaganda, or as reality rather
than imitation: art for today, for the masses, for tomorrow,
and for the elite.

*Hess, Thomas B., and Ashbery, John, eds.   LIGHT, FROM ATEN TO LASER.
Art News Annual XXXV. New York: The Macmillan Co., 1969. Color and
black and white illus.

> Art News Annual, devoted to light as a concept, includes
> essays in which light influences art. "Generation of Light,"
> deals with such contemporary color painters as Kenneth
> Noland, Morris Louis, Hans Hofmann, and Ad Reinhardt. An
> excellent article by Gabriel Laderman analyzes the import-
> tance of light and color in landscape painting.

Homer, William Innes, and Organ, Violet. ROBERT HENRI, AND HIS CIRCLE.
Ithaca, London: Cornell University Press, (c. 1969). xvii, 308 pp. Mostly
black and white illus., diagrams. Bibliography.

> William Homer's analysis of the influence Henri had upon the
> New York School of Art, particularly from 1902-09, and
> his own school from 1909-12, includes color concepts which
> are abstract and poetic rather than concrete and scientific.

Hunter, Sam. AMERICAN ART OF THE 20TH CENTURY. New York: Harry
N. Abrams, Inc., n.d. 487 pp. Color and black and white illus. Bibliography.

> A good summary of the fashionable artistic dictums of our day
> with appropriate descriptions of the meanings and intentions
> in color and design, and the effects upon intentions caused by
> new materials and techniques.

Larkin, Oliver W. ART AND LIFE IN AMERICA. Rev., enl. New York:
Holt, Rinehart and Winston, (c. 1949, 1960). xvii, 559 pp. 482 black and
white illus., 30 color plates.

> Besides having written a fascinating history of art and life in
> America, Larkin documents the color relationships and intentions
> of the American artists. He relates color symbolism to tech-
> nique and execution, as well as to narrative-visual meaning.

Leymarie, Jean. FAUVISM: BIOGRAPHICAL AND CRITICAL STUDY. Translated by James Emmons. Part of "The Taste of Our Time Collection." New
York: Skira, (c. 1959). 166 pp. 71 color plates.

> Simplified but more than adequate history of Fauvism, with
> proper appreciation of the significance of the "color eccentrics"
> who believed fervently in their new school of color.

*Lipschutz, Ilse Hempel. SPANISH PAINTING AND THE FRENCH ROMAN-

TICS. Cambridge, Mass.: Harvard University Press, 1972. xvii, 407 pp. Black and white illus. Bibliography.

Ilse Lipschutz treats color as an emotional and sensuous element in Spanish painting. The author describes carefully the color pallettes that various painters used to achieve various effects. Deep understanding of the Spanish artists including El Greco, Goya, Murillo, Velazquez, and Zurbaran.

*Moholy-Nagy, Sibyl. EXPERIMENT IN TOTALITY. 2nd ed. Cambridge and London: The M.I.T. Press, (c. 1950, 1969). xvii, 259 pp. Illus. (part color). Bibliography

Sibyl's beautiful tribute to her husband, Laszlo, clarifies his position as a great humanist and leader. The Constructionists were most active in their attempt to separate abstract visual elements from personal image-making. Their efforts to create a new interaction between art and science led to experimentation in light, motion. chromatics, and non-illusionistic space. The theories and relationship to light-modulators are provocative and offer a possible stimulus for further investigations. They are quite different in concept and effect from our present-day light boxes.

*Mondrian, Piet. PLASTIC ART AND PURE PLASTIC ART, 1937, AND OTHER ESSAYS, 1941-1943. 3rd ed. Preface by Robert Motherwell. New York: George Wittenborn, Inc., 1945.

The influence of the de Stijl group upon color is still active, perhaps among architects more than painters. Mondrian's essay includes consideration and use of color as the primary hues—red, blue, and yellow. Historically important if not inspirational.

Muller, Joseph-Emile. FAUVISM. New York, Washington: Frederick A. Praeger, Publishers, (c. 1967). 260 pp. Illus. (part color).

Description of color effects achieved by the Fauve painters rather than analysis or even synthesis of concepts. Interesting research and quotations concerning color intentions by Matisse, Gauguin, Vlaminck, and others.

*Praeger Frederick. THE PRAEGER PICTURE ENCYCLOPEDIA OF ART; A COMPREHENSIVE SURVEY OF PAINTING, SCULPTURE, ARCHITECTURE, AND CRAFTS, THEIR METHODS, STYLES, AND TECHNICAL TERMS, FROM THE EARLIEST TIMES TO THE PRESENT DAY. New York: Frederick A. Praeger, Publishers, (c. 1958, 1960). 584 pp. 192 color plates, 416 monochrome illus.

Excellent, general source for color information about palettes, intentions, goals, concepts, and results of artists.

Raynal, Maurice. HISTORY OF MODERN PAINTING FROM BAUDELAIRE TO

BONNARD: THE BIRTH OF A NEW VISION; THE HONFLEUR SCHOOL,
IMPRESSIONISM, NEO-IMPRESSIONISM, SYMBOLISM, POST-IMPRESSION
ISM. 2nd ed. Vol. 1 of 3 vols. Translated by Stuart Gilbert. Introduction
by Herbert Read, historical and biographical notes by Jean Leymarie. Geneva:
Albert Skira, (c. 1949). xxi, 150 pp. Color illus.

_____, et al. HISTORY OF MODERN PAINTING, MATISSE, MUNCH,
ROUAULT, FAUVISM, EXPRESSIONISM; VAN GOGH - GAUGUIN - MATISSE
- MARQUET - VLAMINCK - OERAIN - DUFY - FRIESZ - BRAQUE -
MODERSOHN - KIRCHNER - SCHMIDT-ROTTLUFF - KANDINSKY - JAWLEN-
SKY - MUNCH - HODLER - ENSOR - ROUAULT - NOLDE - WEBER -
KOKOSCHKA - CHAGALL - SOUTINE. Vol. 2 of 3 vols. Translated by Stuart
Gilbert. Introduction by George Schmidt. Translated by Douglas Cooper. Geneva:
Albert Skira, (c. 1950). xxii, 151 pp. Color illus. Biography and bibliography
notices.

_____, et al. HISTORY OF MODERN PAINTING FROM PICASSO TO SURREAL-
ISM; CUBISM - FUTURISM - THE BLUE RIDERS - METAPHYSICAL PAINTING -
DADA - ABSTRACT ART - PURISM - THE REALIST REACTION - THE BAUHAUS -
POETIC PAINTING - SURREALISM. Vol. 3 of 3 vols. Translated by Douglas
Cooper. Geneva: Albert Skira, (c. 1950). 209 pp. Color illus. Biography and
bibliography. Summaries.

> The editors are intelligent, thorough, and rigorously objective in
> their analysis of each artist and his contribution to contemporary
> art. The concepts and techniques of each artist as influenced by
> and influencing other artists, or poets, historians, and events pro-
> vide a balance to the concepts of the artists influenced by their
> perception of nature. Volume 1 covers color concepts of Impres-
> sionism and Neo-Impressionists, including Japanese color prints,
> the color symbolism of Redon, as well as the ideas of the Nabis.
> The color concepts of Fauvism and its aftermath, Die Brucke, and
> finally Expressionism are presented in Vol 12. In the final volume,
> color is examined as it developed from Post-Impressionism and
> Fauvism, through Cubism and reactions to Cubism, and as part of
> the Blue Rider Group. Concepts of Orphism with its harmonious
> organization of colors, the primary colors of the Purists, and the
> palettes of the Magic Realists are examined.

*Rewald, John. THE HISTORY OF IMPRESSIONISM. Rev. and enl. ed. New
York: Museum of Modern Art, (1961). 662 pp. Illus. (part color), portraits,
maps. Biblipgraphy.

> Rewald's engrossing history of Impressionism and its major influence
> upon the art world includes Monet, Renoir, Pissarro, Sisley, Degas,
> Cezanne, and Morisot. Impressionism is almost synonymous with
> light and color; chromaticity rather than tonality. Rewald writes
> analytically and authoritatively of the colors of each artist and his
> contribution to the art of color in painting.

* _____. POST-IMPRESSIONISM FROM VAN GOGH TO GAUGUIN. 2nd
ed. New York: Museum of Modern Art, 1962. 619 pp. Illus. (part color),

maps. Bibliography.

A lovely sequel to THE HISTORY OF IMPRESSIONISM in which Rewald maintains his rigorous analysis, synthesis, and description of the color theories, practice, and psychology of Van Gogh, Seurat, the Symbolists and Anarchists, through the Synthesists' exhibition, including Gauguin and Bonnard. Beautiful descriptions, logical and precise color vocabulary. Excellent sources and notes. First-rate bibliography, mostly in French and German.

*Rheims, Maurice. THE FLOWERING OF ART NOUVEAU. New York: Harry N. Abrams, Inc., n.d. 450 pp. Color and black and white illus., photos.

Color as a psychological expression, and as a physical tool, were dominant factors in the spirit of Art Nouveau. Guimard's use of two-toned colored bricks, and Gaudi's visual mixtures created through his use of glazes and various materials, and his consideration of how light was reflected from surfaces and angles were color thoughts in architecture. Color in painting became the means for reaching a kind of richness and super decoration. Finally, color in objet d'art, glass, and ceramics is probably the culmination of the heightened role of color as perceived in their misty colors, i.e., their layer-cake of many colors. The interaction of color and object related to use is documented in this spirited and lovely work.

*Rickey, George. CONSTRUCTIVISM, ORIGINS AND EVOLUTION. New York: George Braziller, Inc., (c. 1967). xi, 305 pp. Black and white illus. Bibliography. Survey of museum holdings of Constructivist Art, 1963.

The chapter on color is a precise history of color concepts as practiced by those artists influenced by Chevreul, who was instrumental in the Constructivist movement. The discussion of Albers' concerns is most intriguing. Color is constantly referred to, using the vocabulary of color theory throughout the text. Even the black and white reproductions contribute to deeper understanding. Excellent bibliography.

Rosenberg, Harold. THE ANXIOUS OBJECT; ART TODAY AND ITS AUDIENCE. New York: Horizon Press. (c. 1964). 270 pp. Black and white illus.

"Color as a color stroke to begin a painting." Harold Rosenberg covers this color logic as part of his critical analysis of the "Art Scene" including abstract art, collages, assemblages, pop and constructionist. Although color is not his primary goal, the work is generally enlightening in understanding how color is being used today.

_____. THE DE-DEFINITION OF ART; ACTION ART TO POP EARTHWORKS. New York: Horizon Press., (c. 1972). 256 pp. Black and white illus.

Harold Rosenberg touches upon the color theories in practice by
artists included in the categories of Action Art, Pop Art, and
Earthwork Art. Sardonic but informative.

Schonberger, Arno, et al. THE ROCOCO AGE; ART AND CIVILIZATION OF THE
18TH CENTURY. Translated by Daphne Woodward. New York, Toronto, and London:
McGraw-Hill Book Co. Inc., (c. 1959, 1960) Color and black and white illus.

The Rococo Age is primarily concerned with eighteenth-cent-
ury culture as mirrored by art. The authors have a sensitivity to
the color of the times. Their admiration for the delicate chromatic
greys of such painters as Boucher, Fragonard, and Watteau is quite
clear. They attribute much of the new and subtle gradations of color
to the state-manufacturers of tapestries, notably Gobelin and Beau-
vais, where under Chevreul's direction, discoveries and new ad-
vances were made for working with the thousand different shades
and tints of silks and wools.

*Venturi, Lionello. HISTORY OF ART CRITICISM. Translated by Charles Mar-
riott. New York: E. P. Dutton & Co., Inc., 1936. xv, 346 pp. Bibliography.

The chapter on illuminism is particularly meaningful as Lionello
Venturi carefully records the color concepts and particular contributions of Chardin and Fragonard, as well as the other conceptual
contributors to that movement.

* _____ . IMPRESSIONISTS AND SYMBOLISTS: MANET, DEGAS, MONET,
PISSARRO, SISLEY, RENOIR, CEZANNE, SEURAT, GAUGUIN, VAN GOGH,
TOULOUSE-LAUTREC. Translated by Francis Steegmuller. New York and London:
Charles Scribner's Sons, 1950. 244 pp. 217 black and white plates. Bibliography.

Lionello Venturi's critical and appreciative eye describes and
pleasantly analyzes the color of the Impressionists and Symbolists
in his general discourses on their paintings.

Chapter 15

COLOR: KINETICS

Chapter 15

COLOR: KINETICS

*Kepes, Gyorgy, ed. THE NATURE AND ART OF MOTION. New York: George Braziller, (c. 1965). xi, 195 pp. Black and white illus.

Visual ideas, utilizing optical phenomena, kinetic experiences, principles of constancy and invariance in perception, and concepts of illumination are among the categories covered. They create a broad framework of references to which the active mind can respond, finding color-threads of fascinating proportions.

*Moholy-Nagy, Laszlo. VISION IN MOTION. Chicago: Paul Theobald and Co., (c. 1956). 371 pp. Mostly black and white illus.

Laszlo Moholy-Nagy searched constantly for new concepts of visual interaction including ideas of color. His theories began with the hypothesis that two kinds of painters exist, those who tint or use color to study aspects of shape, and those who concentrate upon color and light as such. He also discusses a composite which leads, he feels, to the most important components of painting.

*Popper, Frank. ORIGINS AND DEVELOPMENT OF KINETIC ART. Translated by Stephen Bann. New York: New York Graphic Society, (c. 1968). 272 pp. Illus. (some color). Index.

Popper's book is based upon work done in optics and the science of perception. He traces color and light studies beginning at the turn-of-the-century and reinterprets these concepts focusing upon color theories with the obvious intention of arriving at the goals of the kinetic artists. The ideas are beautifully related, and it is fun to see familiar material altered in this particular way.

Chapter 16

COLOR: PALETTES

Chapter 16

COLOR: PALETTES

Bustanoby, J. H. PRINCIPLES OF COLOR AND COLOR MIXING. New York: McGraw-Hill Book Co., Inc., 1947. xi, 131 pp. 11 plates (part color). Glossary.

This book includes scientific color data (origins), practical application of color, and Bustanoby's aestheitc value of color; excellent color notes on mixing; as well as an abbreviated dictionary of color terms. Mixing of "popular" colors includes recipes for crushed strawberry, delphinium blue, and daffodil. Miscellaneous delight for painters.

*Cennini, Cennino D'Andrea. THE CRAFTSMAN'S HANDBOOK. "Il Libro dell' Arte." Translated by Daniel V. Thompson, Jr. New York: Dover Publications, Inc., (c. 1933, 1960). (This Dover edition, first published in 1954, is an unabridged and unaltered republication of the Thompson translation originally published by Yale University Press in 1933.) xxvii, 142 pp.

Cennino Cennini's 15th-century handbook contains interesting and useful systems for putting into practice color theories. For example, he tells how to "work up" the colors, how to make red for flesh tones, or how to imitate an ultramarine blue for use in frescos. He provides a great deal of vital information about the character of colors as pigments, what natural colors need artificial help, etc.

*Doerner, Max. THE MATERIALS OF THE ARTIST AND THEIR USE IN PAINTING WITH NOTES ON THE TECHNIQUES OF THE OLD MASTERS. Rev. ed. Translated by Eugen Neuhaus. New York: Harcourt, Brace and Co., (c. 1934, 1949). xvi, 435 pp. Black and white illus. Paperbound.

Excellent, readable source of ground preparation and pigment preparation for the painter. Related to a concept of achieving the maximum luminosity reached by the masters. More involved in materials and techniques than many of the books on materials, but one of those wonderful sources.

*Eastlake, Sir Charles Lock. METHODS AND MATERIALS OF PAINTING OF THE GREAT SCHOOLS AND MASTERS, Vol. 1. New York: Dover Publications,

Inc., 1960. (This new Dover edition, first published in 1960, is an unabridged and unaltered republication of the first edition of the work originally published by Longmans, Green and Co. in 1869 under the title, MATERIALS FOR A HISTORY OF OIL PAINTING.) xii, 561 pp.

*_____. METHODS AND MATERIALS OF PAINTING OF THE GREAT SCHOOLS AND MASTERS, Vol. 2. New York: Dover Publications, Inc., 1960. (This new Dover edition, first published in 1960, is an unabridged and unaltered republication of the first edition of the work originally published by Longmans, Green, and Co. in 1869 under the title MATERIALS FOR A HISTORY OF OIL PAINTING.) xiv, 434 pp. Preface. Paperbound.

> The result in Sir Charles Eastlake's investigation of the practice of oil painting from its beginnings is this classic reference describing methods of painting, the origin and purpose as well as the influence upon "its consummate practice." The technical circumstances are essential to understanding color theories in practice, or the reflection of artists theories of color and light in his work. Deals with the technical, "how to" problems of oil painting, fresco, and wax painting, vehicles for paint and preparation, as well as the preparation of materials, professional essays on color harmonies, contrasts, problems of shadows, outline, toning, textures, glazing, etc.

Heberts, Jurt. THE COMPLETE BOOK OF ARTISTS' TECHNIQUES. Translated from the German DIE MALTECHNIKEN. New York, Washington: Frederick A. Praeger, Publishers, (c. 1950). 350 pp. 80 color and black and white illus. Bibliography.

> Color concepts explored and related to various techniques and materials. A balance is developed to produce an equilibrium between particular materials, techniques, and concepts. Discussion of a wide range of materials including those for rock and wall paintings, stained glass, wood cut, charcoal, encaustic, lacquer, and others.

Hiler, Hilaire. NOTES ON THE TECHNIQUE OF PAINTING. Preface by Sir William Rothenstein. New York: Oxford University Press, 1935. vi, 340 pp. Bibliography.

> Excellent chapter on color and pigments including notes related to color perception, classification of colors, pigments, permanency of pigments and their characteristics, and a selection of antique and modern palettes.

*_____. THE PAINTER'S POCKET BOOK OF METHODS AND MATERIALS. Edited by Jan Gordon. Revised by Colin Hayes. London: Faber & Faber, Ltd., (c. 1970). 266 pp. Chart. Glossary.

> A valuable reference book for basic materials, tools, and techniques in painting. Particularly important for the information related to the permanence of materials and its glossary. Basic, basic color theory. Good for beginners in painting.

Homer, William Innes. See: COLOR: ARTISTS' CONCEPTS. Homer, William Innes. SEURAT AND THE SCIENCE OF PAINTING.

Jacobs, Michel. COLOR IN LANDSCAPE PAINTING. New York: The Citadel Press, (c. 1956). 95 pp. Color and black and white illus.

> This book is definitely for the painter; it tends to be subjec-
> tive, but is sensitive while remaining a practical book intended
> to help the painter achieve greater brilliance in his work.
> Michel Jacobs includes many helpful hints toward training
> and developing one's perception.

*Maroger, Jacques. THE SECRET FORMULAS AND TECHNIQUES OF THE MASTERS. Translated by Eleanor Beckham. New York: The Studio Publica-
tions, Inc., (c. 1948). 200 pp. Black and white illus. Bibliography.

> Jacques Maroger's scholarly and sensitive account of the methods
> and formulas of the masters of painting covers tempera, oil,
> lead mediums, lead, and wax as well as preparation of grounds.
> The methods are presented as part of each artist's effort to
> record his ideas on light, color, and form, and show new in-
> ventions and technique developments closely aligned to percep-
> tion and ideology.

*Mayer, Ralph. THE ARTIST'S HANDBOOK OF MATERIALS AND TECH-
NIQUES. New York: The Viking Press, 1940. 561 pp. Diagrams. Bibliography.

> Good technical book with an effort to relate to historical-artis-
> tic ideology, but tells about materials, their strengths or weak-
> nesses. Lucid descriptions for methods of using oil paint, gesso,
> tempera, and other materials, as well as how to mix (make) or
> develop one's own paints and mediums.

Ross, Denman Waldo. THE PAINTER'S PALETTE; A THEORY OF TONE RELA-
TIONS, AN INSTRUMENT OF EXPRESSION. Boston and New York: Houghton Mifflin Co., 1919. viii, 41 pp. Diagrams.

> Denman Ross' color palettes are based upon his concept which
> relates a system of the spectrum band with complementaries in
> corresponding values. It is another way of approaching color
> harmonies and color mixing, but, as he realized, the main pro-
> blem still remains in choosing the paints to mix.

Sargent, Frederick Leroy. A WORKING SYSTEM OF COLOR FOR STUDENTS OF ART AND NATURE. New York: Henry Holt and Co., (c. 1927). iv, 97 pp. Plain and color diagrams.

> The book is easy and fun reading, and would be of particular
> interest to the painter in providing much useful information in
> setting up his palette. For the beginning painter. (See page 123).

Sully, Thomas. HINTS TO YOUNG PAINTERS. Ltd. ed. "An historic treatise on the color expression and painting techniques of American artists of the
Colonial and Federal periods. Reprinted in new format from the original edition
of 1873, with a special introduction by Faber Birren." New York: Reinhold
Publishing Corp., 1965. xxiii, 46 pp. Black and white illus.

> Thomas Sully's palette defines and limits his color expression.
> His sensibility is elegant and primarily deals with portraiture.
> It is a useful book for painters looking for "how-to" informa-
> tion.

Taubes, Frederic. NEW TECHNIQUES IN PAINTING. New York: Dodd,
Mead and Co., 1962. 128 pp. Black and white illus., photos.

> New pigments introduce the need for new techniques. Fred-
> eric Taubes' introduction to modern paint formulations, the
> acrylic emulsions, acrylic, oil paints, new colors, natural and
> synthetic resins, painting media, is all very useful information.

*Taylor, F. A. COLOR TECHNOLOGY FOR ARTISTS, CRAFTSMEN, AND
INDUSTRIAL DESIGNERS. London: Oxford University Press, 1962. xiii, 140
pp. Illus., 9 color plates. Bibliography.

> The book was planned as an introduction to the subject of color
> for the artist and designer. It is a concise, well-written book
> which can be recommended for the technical information it pro-
> vides rather than aesthetic, philosophical attitudes on color.

Thompson, Daniel V. THE MATERIALS OF MEDIEVAL PAINTING. Foreword
by Bernhard Berenson. New Haven: Yale University Press, 1936. 239 pp.

> Technique is explained to develop color understanding within
> the range of hue, value, and intensity. Daniel Thompson's
> description and analysis of the use of particular pigments are
> excellent. His concept of color relates primarily to local
> color and does not approach color as an abstraction, or deal
> with color interaction.

Ward, James. HISTORY AND METHODS OF ANCIENT & MODERN PAINT-
ING; FROM THE EARLIEST TIMES TO THE BEGINNING OF THE RENAIS-
SANCE PERIOD INCLUDING THE METHODS AND MATERIALS OF THE PAINT-
ER'S CRAFT OF ANCIENT & MODERN TIMES. London: Chapman and Hall,
Ltd., 1913. x, 250 pp. 44 black and white full page illus.

> A traditional or conventional concept of color harmony and
> color expression is explored through time, from the earliest
> art to the Renaissance. Color symbolism and local color are
> related to the dictates of culture and the conceptual skills
> developed at that time. Well researched.

Chapter 17

COLOR: PERCEPTION

Chapter 17

COLOR: PERCEPTION

*Arnheim, Rudolf. ART AND VISUAL PERCEPTION; A PSYCHOLOGY OF THE CREATIVE EYE. Berkeley and Los Angeles: University of California Press, 1957, (c. 1954). x, 408 pp. Black and white illus. Bibliography.

> Rudolf Arnheim's comprehension of the relationships between
> modern psychology and the understanding of the creative
> process make this an essential book to our time. His analy-
> sis of color and design related to visual perception stimulates
> the imagination. The chapter on light is excellent, although
> the chapter on the psychological views of color seems arbitrary.

Bart, Sir Montagu Pollock. LIGHT AND WATER; A STUDY OF REFLEXION AND COLOUR IN RIVER, LAKE AND SEA. London: George Bell and Sons, 1903. xii, 115 pp. Black and white illus., photos, diagrams.

> LIGHT AND WATER is a lovely exercise in perception based
> upon the principles of chemistry, psychology, and physics. Per-
> spective, position of the viewer, and weather conditions are
> considered as elements in striving toward color harmony. Limi-
> tation of the book lies in the steps between reality and art, not
> possible to reach in the "how to achieve" rules set by Pollock
> Bart.

*Baudelaire, Charles. THE MIRROR OF ART. Translated and edited by Jonathan Mayne. Garden City, N. Y.: Doubleday and Co. Inc., 1956. xxi, 370 pp. Black and white illus. Paperbound.

> The visual impressions articulated by Baudelaire influenced
> many artists and are still capable of creating new sensory
> effects leading to an appreciation and greater perception of
> color in nature and art. His analytical perception of color
> in nature formed the basis of his color ideas.

*Bell, Clive. ART. New York: Capricorn Books, G. P. Putnam's Sons, 1958. Seventh impression - reprinted by arrangement with Chatto & Windos, Ltd. 190 pp. Preface. Paperbound.

> Clive Bell's concept of "significant form" gently includes

significant color, as he does not make a dichotomy between form and color. He does pursue his idea of art-form and color, as unrelated to science, and indeed limited by science. Beautiful essay.

*Gibson, James J. THE SENSES CONSIDERED AS PERCEPTUAL SYSTEMS. Boston: Houghton Mifflin Co., (c. 1966). xiv, 335 pp. Black and white illus., diagrams. Bibliography.

James Gibson's theory of dynamic perception is primarily concerned with problems encountered while trying to comprehend the world in which we live. Psychological effects of light seem of less importance than perception of pigmentation of surface objects. However, his writings are of extraordinary importance to anyone seriously pursuing color study.

*Gregory, R. L. EYE AND BRAIN; THE PSYCHOLOGY OF SEEING. World University Library Series. New York, Toronto: McGraw-Hill Book Co., (c. 1966). 254 pp. Mostly black and white illus., diagrams, charts, photos. Bibliography. Paperbound.

Seeing as problem solving, an approach to the riddle of how retinal stimulation gives rise to perception of objects. The book contains excellent history of light theories and many perceptual investigations, including experiments related to how we learn to see.

Julesz, Bela. FOUNDATIONS OF CYCLOPEAN PERCEPTION. Chicago and London: The University of Chicago Press, (c. 1971). xiv, 406 pp. Color and black and white illus.

A concept of perception based upon tracing the information flow in the visual system, defining the role of the external eye, and the role of the visual nervous system in forming images. The role of color as the catalyst in defining form in otherwise random patterns of binocular or monocular vision is startling and fascinating.

*Leibowitz, Herschel W. VISUAL PERCEPTION. The Critical Issues in Psychology Series, Melvin H. Marx, General Editor. London: Collier-Macmillan, Ltd., (c. 1965). xii, 177 pp. Diagrams. Paperbound.

Herschel Leibowitz's fascinating interpretation of the representative theoretical and experimental issues involved in visual perception today. Various attributes of color are included as an element in visual perception experimentation.

*Mundle, C. W. K. PERCEPTION: FACTS AND THEORIES. London and New York: Oxford University Press, 1971. 192 pp.

An important and clear document concerning the problems of

perception in their relation to phenomenology and scientific
theories. The most recent substantiated findings concerning
color vision and color perception are recorded. Particularly
informative concerning the function of rods and cones.

Optical Society of America. Committee on Colorimetry. See: COLORIMETRY.
Optical Society of America. Committee on Colorimetry. THE SCIENCE OF
COLOR.

Pirenne, M. H. OPTICS, PAINTING AND PHOTOGRAPHY. London: Cambridge University Press, 1970. xxiv, 199 pp. Black and white illus., diagrams.
Bibliography.

Excellent reading in optics and physiology, of the way we perceive
external objects and reproduce them in art, as well as an analysis
of the problems of perception and the way we perceive paintings.

Pope, Arthur. AN INTRODUCTION TO THE LANGUAGE OF DRAWING AND
PAINTING. Cambridge: Harvard University Press, 1929. 155 pp. Color and
black and white illus. Bibliography.

Pope's work is based upon general theories in visual perception
and upon theories of color and tone relations, particularly
measurement as in colorimetry. The work serves as basis for
understanding representation in terms of drawing and painting.

*Rood, Roland. COLOR AND LIGHT IN PAINTING. Edited by George L.
Stout. New York: Columbia University Press, 1941. viii, 299 pp. Black
and white illus.

A most important book. Roland Rood's basic aesthetics are related
to concepts of sensations. He deals with perceptual problems
such as arbitrary values and constancy, light and shadow as concepts, broken color and luster, additive and subtractive mixes,
local color, and shadow. His point of view, while scientifically
oriented, remains personal because of his unique interests.

Seitz, William. C. THE RESPONSIVE EYE. (The Museum of Modern Art in collaboration with the City Art Museum of St. Louis, the Contemporary Art
Council of the Seattle Art Museum, the Pasadena Art Museum and the Baltimore Museum of Art.) Rochester, N.Y.: Hoyt Corp., 3rd print., 1966 (c.
1965). 51 pp. Plates (part color).

William Seitz writes about color painters who are making important contributions to our visual perception and awareness.
He makes no effort to evaluate their work.

Sheppard, Joseph J., Jr. HUMAN COLOR PERCEPTION; A CRITICAL STUDY
OF THE EXPERIMENTAL FOUNDATION. New York: American Elsevier Pub-
lishing Co., 1968. xvii, 192 pp. Black and white illus., graphs, charts.
Bibliography.

A scientific introduction to an experimental foundation for

human color perception. Three fields of color vision are
considered: colorimetry, visual biophysics, and visual psycho-
physics. Although technical for the artist-layman, it is an
important book to consider for the artist building concepts
about color.

Swartz, Robert J., ed. PERCEIVING, SENSING, AND KNOWING; A BOOK
OF READINGS FROM TWENTIETH-CENTURY SOURCES IN THE PHILOSOPHY
OF PERCEPTION. Introduction by Robert Swartz. Garden City, N.Y.:
Anchor Books, Doubleday & Co., Inc., (c. 1965). xxii, 538 pp. Bibli-
ography. Paperbound.

Concepts dealing with the nature of sense-perception, phenomenal-
ism and causal theory. Empirical knowledge, as based upon sense-
evidence, is also considered in this collection of essays. A serious
student of color theory should be aware of the contemporary philosophical thinking in this area.

Vernon, Magdalen Dorothea, ed. EXPERIMENTS IN VISUAL PERCEPTION;
SELECTED READINGS. Baltimore: Penguin Books, Inc., (1968). 443 pp.
Black and white illus., diagrams. References at end of each reading. Paper-
bound.

A basic book that includes the classic authors in the field of
visual perception. Helpful to the student of color interested in
in knowing more of why and how he sees color rather than
merely what he sees. Includes Koffka, Gibson, Ittelson, Leibowitz, and Piaget.

Chapter 18

COLOR: PSYCHOLOGY

Chapter 18

COLOR: PSYCHOLOGY

*Arnheim, Rudolf. TOWARD A PSYCHOLOGY OF ART. Berkeley and Los
Angeles: University of California Press., (c. 1966, 1967). 369 pp. Black
and white illus. Index.

> Rudolf Arnheim's essays were written between the 1940's and the
> present. Gestalt psychology and the philosophy of such people
> as Wolfgang Kohler and William James form the basis of his psychol-
> ogy of art, which in turn effects his thoughts about color per-
> ception and expression.

Bernstein, Martha. COLOUR IN ART AND DAILY LIFE. Translated by R.
Granger Watkin. New York: Robert M. Watkin. New York: Robert M.
McBride & Co., 1928. xii, 241 pp.

> An effort to deal with the psychological effects of color in a prag-
> matic way, as though the effects of color were constant and not
> affected by changing social points of view. However, the exami-
> nation of each color and its specific meaning at different times to
> different artists can heighten one's sense of color and provide a
> way of reflecting one's unique experiences and character.

Birren, Faber. COLOR PSYCHOLOGY AND COLOR THERAPY; A FACTUAL
STUDY OF THE INFLUENCE OF COLOR ON HUMAN LIFE. New Hyde Park,
N.Y.: University Books, Inc., (c. 1950, 1961). xv, 302 pp. Black and
white illus., photos. Bibliography.

> Color psychology and color therapy presented in a breezy manner,
> combining superstitions with myths, bits and pieces of science in
> a journalistic sort of way. Fascinating reading, but it leaves one
> with a curious sensation of words running through one's fingers.

Cheskin, Louis. COLORS, WHAT THEY CAN DO FOR YOU. New York:
Liveright Publishing Corp., (c. 1947). 333 pp. Color illus.

> Although some attempt is made to relate color to scientific
> theories and to deal with color as pigment, Louis Cheskin's
> basic attitude toward color is an emotional one. He deals
> with color as it expresses personality traits in various human

situations and activities.

Danger, Eric Paxton. HOW TO USE COLOR TO SELL. Foreword by Faber Birren. Boston: Cahners Books, Inc., 1969, (c. 1968). (London edition published in 1968 has title: USING COLOUR TO SELL.) 224 pp. Bibliography.

A great deal of perceptual information concerning the psychology of color written for marketing people, or for those who want to know how to use color and to achieve certain effects in easy, secure steps. Questionable idea.

*Ehrenzweig, Anton. THE HIDDEN ORDER OF ART; A STUDY IN THE PSYCHOLOGY OF ARTISTIC IMAGINATION. Berkeley and Los Angeles: University of California Press., (c. 1967, 1969, 1971). 306 pp. Black and white illus. Glossary. Refererences. Paperbound.

This classic on the psychology of artistic creativity deals provocatively with color conventions and their problems, such as "local color," "color matching," and "arbitrary color combination" (as in the Fauves). He includes thoughts on color as affected by form, by color in space (Bezold, but not illumination), by principles of color interaction, by color serialization., and by the effects of consonance and dissonance.

*Gombrich, E. H. ART AND ILLUSION; A STUDY IN THE PSYCHOLOGY OF PICTORIAL REPRESENTATION. The A. W. Mellon Lectures in the Fine Arts, 1956, National Gallery of Art, Washington, Bollingen Series, vol. 35, no. 5. New York: Pantheon Books, (c. 1960). xxxi, 466 pp. 319 illus. (Mostly black and white). Bibliography. Paperbound.

The author's concern with color is related to theories of visual perception, Gestalt psychology, more conventional ideas of local color, pure color, and some mystical inquiries into meanings in light and darkness. These general theories of visual perception are important to any study of color.

Greenberg, Clement. ART AND CULTURE; CRITICAL ESSAYS. Boston: Beacon Press, (c. 1961, 1965, 1967). x, 278 pp.

Clement Greenberg writes intelligently, and includes the role of color in the work of various artists whom he describes as having special influences in the art world. He discusses the color theories of the painter Monet and the psychological effect he had upon American artists.

*Kandinsky, Wassily. CONCERNING THE SPIRITUAL IN ART, AND PAINTING IN PARTICULAR, 1912. Translated by Michael Sadleir. New York: George Wittenborn, Inc., (c. 1947, 1955). (First published in English as: THE ART OF SPIRITUAL HARMONY.) 93 pp. Black and white illus., photo, diagrams. Bibliography. Paperbound.

_____. THE ART OF SPIRITUAL HARMONY. Translated with introduc-·
tion by M.T.H. Sadleir. London: Constable and Co., Ltd., 1914. xxvii,
112 pp. 9 plates, 3 diagrams.

> Wassily Kandinsky's passionate love for color stimulated his
> investigation into the multifold meanings of color. His paint-
> ings and writings reflect his inner struggle and grasp of the
> relationship between color and mysticism. Important contri-
> bution to the painter.

*Koffka, Kurt. PRINCIPLES OF GESTALT PSYCHOLOGY. New York: Har-
court, Brace & World, Inc., (c. 1963, 1935). xi, 720 pp. Illustrations, diagrams. Bibliography. Paperbound.

> PRINCIPLES OF GESTALT PSYCHOLOGY deals with important
> psychological phenomena relevant to color concepts, particularly
> in the perception of shape, proximity and equality, figure and
> ground, and major problems of constancy.

Kohler, Wolfgang. GESTALT PSYCHOLOGY. New York: H. Liveright,
1929. New York: Mentor Books, (c. 1947)., 403 pp. Illus. Bibliography,
at end of each chapter. Paperbound.

> Good basic introduction to Gestalt psychology. Gestalt psy-
> chology postulates the theory, contrasted to aesthetics, that con-
> siders color and light as part of a concept of the sensory organiza-
> tional system necessary to forming images.

Malraux, Andre. THE PSYCHOLOGY OF ART; THE TWILIGHT OF THE AB-
SOLUTE. Vol. 3. Translated by Stuart Gilbert. The Bollingen Series, vol.
24. New York: Pantheon Books, Inc., (c. 1950). 275 pp. Black and white
illus., color plates. Index.

> Important to the student of color as Andre Malraux's erudition
> and pursuit of meaning in art relates color perception to the
> realization of the meaning of the art object. He articulates
> visual metaphors in a precise yet poetic manner, comparing the
> use of light and color on many levels among numerous artists.

Phillipps, Lisle March. FORM AND COLOUR. London: Duckworth, 1925.
xv, 294 pp.

> Psychological effects of color perceived in nature and in Eastern
> (especially Byzantine) and Western architecture. Lisle Phillips
> describes the psychological and philosophical effects of color as
> it is reflected in the art of various cultures.

Chapter 19

COLOR: SYSTEMS

Chapter 19

COLOR: SYSTEMS

Cleland, Thomas Maitland. THE MUNSELL COLOR SYSTEM; A PRACTICAL DESCRIPTION OF, WITH SUGGESTIONS FOR ITS USE. Baltimore: Munsell Color Co., Inc., 1937. 21 pp. Diagrams (part color).

> Deals with color notation and standardization developing the
> color wheel into a color tree, with a neat place for each
> color, tint, or shade.

Container Corp. of America. COLOR HARMONY MANUAL; 949 DIFFERENT COLOR CHIPS IN REMOVABLE FORM ARRANGED AND NOTATED ACCORD-ING TO THE ORIGINAL SYSTEM OF WILHELM OSTWALD. Supplements: "Ex-planatory Text to Fourth Edition," "Color Names Dictionary," "Directory of Owners, ninth ed.," "Table of Reflection Factors." Chicago: Container Corp-oration Portfolio. Undated, variously paged.

> The color harmony manual is equipped with an operational
> manual describing the possible uses and ways of using the
> Ostwald system.

Grosser, Maurice. THE PAINTER'S EYE. New York: Mentor Books, (c. 1951, 1955). (This is a reprint of the original hardcover edition published by Rinehart and Co., Inc.) 192 pp. Black and white illus. Preface. Paperbound.

> Maurice Grosser's color approach deals with additive and sub-
> tractive mixes of pigments. He touches upon Ostwald's systems
> of color scales and ends with Dr. Herbert Ives' system of the
> subtractive mixture of the minus colors.

Harris, Moses. THE NATURAL SYSTEM OF COLOURS 1766: A FACSIMILE EDI-TION OF WHAT IS PERHAPS THE RAREST KNOWN BOOK IN THE LITERATURE OF COLOR, with Historical Notes and Commentary by Faber Birren. Privately Printed in a limited Edition in 1963. Distributed by Whitney Library of Design, New York. 8 pp. Color and black and white illus.

> Moses Harris presents a color circle in full hue, describes a system
> of mixing colors based upon the spectral colors, and relates a con-
> cept of "primitive" and "mediate" colors to colors of natural objects.
> The book in its thoughtfulness is delightful.

Color: Systems

Jacobson, Egbert. BASIC COLOR, AN INTERPRETATION OF THE OSTWALD COLOR SYSTEM. Chicago: Paul Theobald, (c. 1948). 207 pp. Color and black and white illus. Bibliography.

Egbert Jacobson's interpretation of Ostwald's color system appeared at a time when to categorize and simplify was among the highest of achievements. Industry was most acceptable to the cataloging of colors and to Jacobson's color tree. Artists have been generally impatient with any efforts to catalog and organize pigment mixes, especially with the emphasis on black to darken colors, as shown in Jacobson's charts. He also defines harmonious color combinations and present methods for achieving them. It is unfortunate, but probably natural, that Jacobson did not develop his ideas related to the psychology of color sensation. Excellent color bibliography.

Munsell, Albert Henry. A COLOR NOTATION. "An illustrated system defining all colors and their relations by measured scales of hue, value, and chroma." 9th ed., edited and rearranged. Baltimore, Md.: Munsell Color Co., Inc., 1941. 74 pp. Frontispiece, illus., color plates, diagrams.

COLOR NOTATION is a summary of Munsell's notation or description and synthesis of his thinking as he developed conceptually toward his color tree. Probably significant today as the pioneer of color standardization, and is important to industry but less to the creative person.

_____. A GRAMMAR OF COLOR; A BASIC TREATISE IN THE COLOR SYSTEM OF ALBERT H. MUNSELL. Edited by Faber Birren. New York, Cincinnati, London, Toronto, Melbourne: Van Nostrand Reinhold Co., (c. 1969). 96 pp. Illus. (part color), diagrams.

Albert Munsell's concept of ideal balance is based upon abstract principles of design and a visual organization of color in his color tree, but is unrelated to color principles such as simultaneous contrast as an occurence between viewer and physical color.

_____. MUNSELL BOOK OF COLOR; DEFINING, EXPLAINING, AND ILLUSTRATING THE FUNDAMENTAL CHARACTERISTICS OF COLOR. Baltimore: Munsell Color Co., Inc., 1929. 42 pp. 26 color plates (part double). Diagrams.

A revision of "Atlas of the Munsell Color System." Color perceived as hue, value, and intensity and organized into a system called the "Munsell system." The basis of his color system is the color sphere. An aid to color notation and nomenclature.

Ostwald, Wilhelm. THE COLOR PRIMER: A BASIC TREATISE ON THE COLOR SYSTEM OF WILHELM OSTWALD. Edited by Faber Birren. New York, Cincinnati, London, Toronto, Melbourne: Van Nostrand Reinhold Co. 96 pp. 8 color plates, diagrams.

Wilhelm Ostwald's primer is helpful providing one accepts black
and white as a physical and primary way of tinting and shading
colors.   However, his concept of visual and graphic organization is lucid and helpful in grasping principles of hue, value,
and intensity in their shifting interacting roles.   Ostwald's concern is with the attributes of color that relate to color-paint
mixtures.

Sargent, Frederick Leroy.   A WORKING SYSTEM OF COLOR FOR STUDENTS
OF ART AND NATURE.   New York: Henry Holt and Co., (c. 1927).   iv, 97
pp.   Color and black and white illus.

Colors are considered primarily as pigment, or paint, with directions for mixing tones and shades.   In Sargent's book, hues are
analyzed according to normal vision, and also related to the color
of things (local color).   A method for a color shorthand is sug-
gested, which may be helpful to a landscape painter with a
short memory.   (See page 105.)

Smith, Charles N. STUDENT HANDBOOK OF COLOR.   New York: Reinhold
Publishing Corp., (c. 1965).   95 pp.   Color and black and white illus.   Diagrams.   Bibliography.

Charles Smith skims across solid scientific material to present
his book of color: How we see color and what we see are
related to the psychological color-solid of Wilhelm Ostwald.
He sets up a system of colors from this solid.

Chapter 20

COLOR: THEORIES

Chapter 20

COLOR: THEORIES

*Bezold, Dr. William Von. THE THEORY OF COLOR; IN ITS RELATION TO ART AND ART-INDUSTRY. Rev., enl. Translated by S. R. Koehler. Introduction and notes by Edward C. Pickering. Boston: L. Prang and Color, (c. 1876). xxxiii, 274 pp. Illus. (part color), diagrams. Bibliography.

> Dr. Bezold's work is still most important as a source book of
> other theories and as an introduction to the "Bezold Effect."
> He critically examines the physiology of color as developed by
> Helmholtz, Maxwell, Brucke, and Chevreul, and attempts to
> rebut Goethe's theory of color. His own work is based upon
> the behavior of objects in light, or light interrupted by objects.

Broad, C. D. SCIENTIFIC THOUGHT. London: Routledge & Kegan Paul Ltd., (1923, 1927, 1949). 555 pp.

> The author's philosophical consideration of the traditional con-
> cepts of time, space, and motion are developed from the edu-
> cated, common sense point of view. He examines the color wave
> length theory with reservation, declaring it oversimplified.

*Chevreul, M. E. THE PRINCIPLES OF HARMONY AND CONTRAST OF COL-ORS AND THEIR APPLICATIONS TO THE ARTS. New York, Amsterdam, and London: Reinhold Publishing Corp., 1967. (Based on the first English edition of 1854 as translated from the first French edition of 1839: DE LA LOI DU CONTRASTE SIMULTANE DES COLEURS with a special introduction and explanatory notes by Faber Birren.) 256 pp. Mostly color illus., photos.

> The contrast and harmony of color principles are related to prob-
> lems of color vision and are basic concepts to the color theory
> of Impressionism, Neo-, or Post-Impressionism and contemporary
> optical painters. Theoretical work has practical meaning for paint-
> ers, carpet makers, tapestry designers, and stained glass artists.
> Chevreul's preferences in visual mixes, harmonies, and contrasts
> are highly subjective, but he is refreshing in his candor about
> his own preferences.

*Evans, Ralph Merrill. AN INTRODUCTION TO COLOR. New York: John Wiley & Sons, Inc.; London: Chapman & Hall, Ltd., 1948. x, 340 pp. 15 color plates.

Black and white illus., diagrams, charts, graphs. Bibliography.

> An important book for any student of color. It is a thought-
> ful and thought provoking book. Explores the physics, physi-
> ology, and psychology of color (See page 64.)

Goethe, Johann Wolfgang von. THEORY OF COLOURS. Translated by Sir
Charles Lock Eastlake. London: John Murray, 1840. (This "O-P Book" is an
authorized reprint of the original edition, produced by Microfilm-Xerography
by University Microfilms, Inc., Ann Arbor, Mich., 1963.) xlviii, 423 pp.

> Sir Charles Eastlake's translation, the first in English, is still
> the most comprehensive of Goethe's color concepts and experi-
> ments.

_____. See: COLOR: THEORIES. Matthaei, Rupprecht, ed. GOETHE'S
COLORY THEORY, and "Color Aesthetics."

_____. See: COLOR: THEORIES. Schindler, Maria, and Merry, Eleanor
C. PURE COLOR: TOWARDS A NEW CULTURE.

Harris, Moses. See: COLOR: SYSTEMS. Harris, Moses. THE NATURAL
SYSTEM OF COLOURS 1766: A FACSIMILE EDITION OF WHAT IS PERHAPS
THE RAREST KNOWN BOOK IN THE LITERATURE OF COLOR.

Hellman, Hal. THE ART AND SCIENCE OF COLOR. Illus. by Mark Binn.
New York: McGraw-Hill Book Co., (c. 1967). 175 pp. Illus. (some color),
diagrams. Bibliography.

> A primer of color in which Hal Hellman deals superficially with
> the phsycis of light, photosynthesis, luminescence, visual mix-
> tures, simultaneous contrast, and color psychology.

*Helmholtz, Hetmann Ludwig Ferdinand von. PHYSIOLOGICAL OPTICS. Ed-
ited by James P. C. Southall. Translation from the third German edition. 3
vols. Menasha, Wis.: The Optical Society of America, 1924, 1925. Vol. I,
xvii, 482 pp.; vol. II, "The Sensations of Vision," viii, 480 p.; vol. III, "The
Perceptions of Vision," x, 736 pp. Black and white illus., diagrams, charts.
Bibliography.

> A pioneer in physiological optics, these three volumes provide an
> exhausting amount of information on seeing and perceiving color.
> Volume I pertains primarily to the anatomical description of the
> eye, physiological optics, and dioptrics of the eye. Volume II
> deals with the sensation of vision, color mixing, prismatic colors,
> color phenomena, and theories of vision. Volume III deals with
> perception of vision, eye movements, monocular field of vision,
> and binocular double vision. Considered a classic.

*Hering, Ewald. OUTLINES OF A THEORY OF THE LIGHT SENSE. Transla-
ted by Leo M. Hurvich and Dorothea Jameson. Cambridge, Mass.: Harvard

University Press, 1964. xxvii, 317 pp. Black and white illus. Diagrams. References.

Ewald Hering's theories developed in the 1860's are surprisingly up to date, particularly his reasoning that the visual system must be conceptualized as tissues of interrelated rather than independent elements. His work with brightness and color contrast is particularly important to students of color today.

*Ladd-Franklin, Christine, Ph.D. COLOUR AND COLOUR THEORIES. New York: Harcourt, Brace & Co.; London: Kegan Paul, Tranch, Trubner & Co., 1929. xv, 287 pp. Illus. (some color). Glossary.

Ladd-Franklin's theory of the color-sensations is basically a continuous argument against the separation of the color theories of Helmholtz and of Hering. Dr. Ladd-Franklin's theory is based upon the evolution of our color sense and relates stages of its development to zones of the retina. Her theory relates a chemical reaction to light within rods and cones to transmitting nerve currents to the brain, thereby producing color sensation.

Leepa, Allen. THE CHALLENGE OF MODERN ART. Rev., ed. Foreword by Herbert Read. New York: Thomas Yoseloff, Inc., (c. 1949, 1957). lxxv, 256 pp. Black and white illus., photos, diagrams.

Allen Leepa's functional analysis includes color theories that insist upon the mutual interaction of medium and ideas. He postulates that without emotional intensity related to color the painting will have little meaning.

Leonardo da Vinci. See: COLOR: ARTIST'S CONCEPTS. Goldscheider, Ludwig. LEONARDO DA VINCI: THE ARTIST.

*Luckiesh, Matthew. COLOR AND ITS APPLICATION. 2nd ed., enl. New York: D. Van Nostrand Co., 1921. xii, 419 pp. Illus., diagrams. References.

Important scientific document and source book covering all important color theories until 1921, including simultaneous contrast, color in lighting, mobile color, color photometry. Presents color vision theories of Young-Helmholtz, Hering, Ladd-Franklin, Eldridge-Green, Aristotle, Benham, Fechner, Ives, Luckiesh, Munsell, Maxwell, Purkinje, Ogden Rood, Tyndall, Leonardo da Vinci, and Wundt.

*Matthaei, Rupprecht, ed. GOETHE'S COLOR THEORY. Translated by Herb Aach. New York, Cincinnati, Toronto, London, Melbourne: Van Nostrand Reinhold Co., (c. 1970). 275 pp. Color and black and white illus. With a complete facsimile reproduction of Charles Eastlake's 1820 translation of the "didactic part" of the color theory.

Goethe's theories have continued to inspire students of color, particularly in his perception of natural phenomena. He experienced all light as color, perceived the nuances of colored light, the effects of half-light and double-shadows. Because of his sensitive awareness, Goethe perceived color and light as "modes of appearances and attributes of light and color," although his vocabulary was poetic and personal, it was not our current scientific one to describe the same phenomena. His optical experiments are recorded and well illustrated. The new edition is altogether a treasure.

Mueller, Robert E. THE SCIENCE OF ART; THE CYBERNETICS OF CREATIVE COMMUNICATION. New York: The John Day Co., (c. 1967). 352 pp. Drawings by author. References.

Robert Mueller discusses the rudimentary hierarchy of color combinations related to the sensory and chemical capacity of the eye to light and color. He recognizes the minimal importance of any perfect scientific theory of color to the artist. Also pursues relationship between color chords and musical chords, noteworthy but not satisfactory.

*Newton, Sir Isaac. OPTICKS: OR A TREATISE OF THE REFLECTIONS, REFRACTIONS, INFLECTIONS, & COLOURS OF LIGHT Foreword by Albert Einstein, introduction by Sir Edmund Whittaker, preface by I. Bernard Cohen, analytical table of contents prepared by Duane H. K. Roller. New York: Dover Publications, Inc., (c. 1952). (Based on the fourth edition, London, 1730. Dover edition is republication of the work published by G. Bell and Sons, Ltd. in 1931.) Black and white illus., tables, diagrams. Paperbound.

Sir Isaac Newton investigated all aspects of light. His writings include experiments with the spectrum, observations concerning the reflections, refractions and colors of thin transparent bodies, and observations concerning the inflections of rays of light and the resulting colors. Essential basic study.

*Ronchi, Vasco. THE NATURE OF LIGHT; AN HISTORICAL SURVEY. Translated by V. Barucas. Cambridge, Mass.: Harvard University Press, 1971. xii, 288 pp. Color and black and white illus.

The nature of light is a history of optics. Vasco Ronchi is well aware of the role that light and optics has played in the development of logical concepts concerning color. Excellent source book. Includes Descartes, Euclid, Fresnel, Goethe, Helmholtz, Huygens, Newton, Plato, St. Thomas Aquinas, Young, and Leonardo da Vinci.

Schindler, Maria, and Merry, Eleanor C. PURE COLOR: TOWARDS A NEW CULTURE, NOS. 5, 6, 7, PT. 1--GOETHE'S THEORY OF COLOUR APPLIED, PT. 2--PAINTING AND IMAGINATION, PT. 3--EXTRACTS FROM GOETHE'S SCIENTIFIC WORK. London: New Culture Publications, 1946. 270 pp. Mostly color plates.

This translation of Goethe's color theories emphasizes the aesthetic, moral, and poetic rather than the scientific. It seems in many ways to capture the particular and unique qualities of Goethe's theories that stressed man in relation to nature rather than in relation to science. Prismatic colors, grey, physiological colors, color combinations, single colors, light and darkness, as well as the balanced color circle are covered.

Teddington, Eng. VISUAL PROBLEMS OF COLOR: Symposium on the Visual Problems of Colour which was held at the National Physical Laboratory from 23rd to 25th September, 1957. 2 vols. vol. I, 395 pp.; vol. II, 367 pp. Black and white illus., charts, graphs, diagrams. Bibliography.

Collection of articles by more than forty scientists reporting on their researches into visual problems of color. Volume I covers retinal chemistry and the physiology of vision, visual pigments, brightness matching and color matching, color vision, and the natural image. Volume II covers subjective color measurement, the electro-physiological aspect of vision, and color theories. Highly technical and would be of particular interest to the scientist and psychologist.

Wright, William David. See: COLOR: VISION. Wright, William David. THE RAYS ARE NOT COLORED; ESSAYS ON THE SCIENCE OF VISION AND COLOUR.

Wyzecki, Gunter, and Stiles, W. S. COLOR SCIENCE; CONCEPTS AND METHODS, QUANTITATIVE DATA AND FORMULAS. New York, London, Sydney: John Wiley and Sons, Inc., (c. 1967). xiv, 628 pp. Black and white illus., tables, diagrams. Bibliography.

A collection of concepts and methods, quantitative data, and formulas bearing on color science directed to the colorimetrist, or those primarily concerned with color problems in industry and research. However, a valuable source book for the theories developed by Munsell, Helmholtz, Schrodinger, Bezold-Brucke, or Weber-Fechner.

*Young, Thomas. "The Bakerian Lecture on the Theory of Light & Colors." THE WAVE THEORY OF LIGHT; MEMORIES BY HUYGENS, YOUNG, AND FRESNEL. Edited by Henry Crew. New York, Cincinnati: American Book Co., (c. 1900). 48 pp. Charts. Black and white illus.

Strongly supportive of Newton's optical observations and proceeds to develop further his theory for the undulatory system of light, confirmed by an analysis of colors of striated substances. Scientific but important for understanding this aspect of color.

Chapter 21

COLOR: VISION

Chapter 21

COLOR: VISION

Albers, Josef. See: COLOR: EDUCATION. Albers, Josef. INTERACTION OF COLOR.

*Arnheim, Rudolf. VISUAL THINKING. Berkeley and Los Angeles: University of California Press., (c. 1969). xi, 338 pp. Black and white illus., drawings, diagrams. Bibliography.

> The writing is brilliant and moves easily from the world of the scientists to that of the artists. Rudolf Arnheim weaves visual ideas beginning with simple perception to the complex order of visual thinking. Color has its unique place in this order, and the artist needs the insights presented here.

Bergmans, J. SEEING COLOR. New York: The Macmillan Co., 1960. Translated by T. Holmes.

> The book gives a concise, general treatment of the problem of color-vision, by making use of a "colour map or triangle." While interesting in theory, the book is an over-simplification of color perception.

Gregory, Albert. COLOR IN LINE. New Haven, Conn.: Yale University Press, 1960. 31 pp. Color illus.

> Albert Gregory suggests that this is a color book to look at. The design remains constant while the color changes from page to page. Although the plates have been silk-screened and have the acetate overlays, the interaction seems strangely familiar and black-and-whitish rather than chromatic.

Harlan, Calvin. VISION AND INVENTION; A COURSE IN ART FUNDAMENTALS. Englewood Cliffs, N.J.: Prentice-Hall, Inc., (c. 1970). xiii, 203 pp. Color and black and white illus., diagrams.

> The chapter on color may be helpful to the art teacher of the young. Calvin Harlan's approach to color is simple and direct. He deals with chemistry and origins of pigment and how to apply pigment to a surface on canvas. He treats the psychological properties of color comparatively, and includes color systems, simul-

taneous contrast, and optics.

*Judd, Deane B., and Wyszecki, Gunter. COLOR IN BUSINESS, SCIENCE, AND INDUSTRY. 2nd ed. New York and London: John Wiley & Sons, Inc., (c. 1952, 1963). x, 500 pp. Black and white illus., tables, graphs. Bibliography.

> Similar to the first edition but with new information in the development of colorimetry and new insights into color perception. The chapter, "Object-Color Perception in Complicated Scenes," is especially meaningful to the artist. Good bibliography for color vision and colorimetry.

*Katz, David. THE WORLD OF COLOUR. Translated by R. B. MacLeod and C. W. Fox. London: K. Paul, Trench, Trubner, 1935; New York: Johnson Reprint (1970). 300 pp.

> Excellent reference book for the student of color interested in the psychology of modes of appearance of color and the phenomenology of illumination. Superb summary of available studies to 1935 of color constancy and color contrast, and of the problems and theories of light and color. Includes the theories of Brucke, Fechner, Goethe, Helmholtz, Hering, Matthaei, and Purkinje, among other excellent sources.

Kepes, Gyorgy, ed. EDUCATION OF VISION. Vision and Value Series. New York: George Braziller, Inc., (c. 1965). vii, 233 pp. Black and white illus.

> A book to be read in conjunction with those on color theories in order to relate the study of vision as a cognitive power to the way concepts of color may be developed.

_____. LANGUAGE OF VISION, with Introductory essays by S. Giedion and S. I. Hayakawa. Chicago: Paul Theobald, 1951. 228 pp. Black and white illus.

> Color as a dynamic element of visual expression with its definite place in the physiological field of study has a major role in Kepes' book. His concepts are related and based upon the theories of Leonardo da Vinci, Goethe, Schopenhauer, Chevreul, and Ostwald.

_____, ed. THE VISUAL ARTS TODAY. Middletown, Conn.: Wesleyan University Press, (c. 1960). 272 pp. Black and white illus.

> Color is considered as a physical and psychological reality, and while not the dominant theme, it is an important note throughout this collection of essays.

Le Grand, Yves. FORM AND SPACE VISION. Revised and translated by Michel Millodot and Gordon G. Heath. Bloomington and London: Indiana University Press, (1967). xv, 367 pp. Black and white illus., graphs, diagrams and charts.

Le Grand is concerned with the physical and physiological factors in the vision of details, forms, movements, and depth. The role of binocular vision in the structure of visual space is explored. It is a needed complement to any study of color and vision.

*_____. LIGHT, COLOUR AND VISION. Translated by R. W. G. Hunt, et al. New York: Dover Publications, Inc., 1957. xiii, 512 pp. Illus., tables. Bibliography.

Light, color, and vision from the physiological, optical point of view. Highly technical, experimental, and rewarding description of the "essential ways in which the optics of the eye and the properties of the retina provide us with our perception of the universe; including form, detail, color, depth, and movement." Experimental information includes data about radiant energy, visual receptors, photometric qualities, colorimetry, thresholds, and spatial interaction. Theories of vision include anatomy, photochemistry, and electrophysiology of the retina. Excellent scientific bibliography. Includes references to Dalton, Brucke, Fresnel, G. A. Fry, Hering, Helmholtz, Ives, Deane B. Judd, and Purkinje.

Luckiesh, Matthew, and Moss, Frank K. SEEING; A PARTNERSHIP OF LIGHTING AND VISION. Baltimore: Williams & Wilkins Co., 1931. vii, 241 pp. Black and white illus. References. Supplement.

The relationship between lighting and vision is systematically analyzed and viewed from many sides, as Luckiesh develops his theme of our half-seeing world. He discusses the way the eye services us, the things the eye can do, and the need for good lighting, as well as what good lighting is. Many visual illusions and problems are considered.

*_____. VISUAL ILLUSIONS, THEIR CAUSES, CHARACTERISTIC APPLICA-TIONS. New York: D. Van Nostrand Co., 1922. ix, 252 pp. Illus., diagrams. References. (Published by Dover Publications [1965] with a new introduction by William H. Ittelson.) Paperbound.

Matthew Luckiesh's selected experiments in the science of color intended for those in the arts is a classic. Light and color, production of color, color mixture, color terminology, the analysis and history of vision and concepts of lighting are among his subjects. Sources are traditional and inclusive. Aristotle, Bernham, Helmholtz, Hering, Fechner, Ladd-Franklin, Purkinje, Chevreul, Leonardo da Vinci, and Brucke are among those whose contributions are important to the artist.

Teevan, Richard C., and Birney, Robert C. eds. COLOR VISION: AN EN-

DURING PROBLEM IN PSYCHOLOGY. Princeton, Toronto, New York, London: D. Van Nostrand Co., Inc., (c. 1961). viii, 214 pp. Introduction, diagrams, charts. Paperbound.

> A good basic primer, particularly for the classic theorists of color vision. Includes excerpts from work by Thomas Young, Hetmann von Helmholtz, Ewald Hering, Adolf Rick, Christine Ladd-Franklin, and up to Edwin Land and Charles E. Osgood.

*Wright, William David. THE RAYS ARE NOT COLORED; ESSAYS ON THE SCIENCE OF VISION AND COLOUR. New York: American Elsevier Publishing Co., Inc., (c. 1967). x, 153 pp. Illus. (some color), graphs.

> A most sensitive collection of lectures by a scientist. He considers the various aspects of light and color from a scientific view related to the psychology of color. David Wright considers the craftsmen, the artist, and problems of subjectivity and craft in a rather wondrous way.

Chapter 22

COLOR: VOCABULARY

Chapter 22

COLOR: VOCABULARY

Berlin, Brent, and Kay, Paul. BASIC COLOR TERMS; THEIR UNIVERSALITY
AND EVOLUTION. Berkeley and Los Angeles: University of California Press,
(c. 1969). xi, 178 pp. Black and white illus., diagrams.

> The evolution and universality of basic color; perceptually and
> linguistically an effort to reach agreement upon the ability of
> various ethnic groups to discriminate among colors and a relation-
> ship to a common vocabulary.

Maerz, Aloys, and Paul, M. Rea. A DICTIONARY OF COLOR. New York:
McGraw-Hill Book Co. Inc., 1930. vii, 207 pp. 56 color plates.

> The dictionary is based upon the effort to standardize color
> names and their color sensations. Contains the history of color
> standardization, includes textile names, traditional names,
> scientific names, as well as common errors in color-name usage,
> and color definitions.

Mayer, Ralph. A DICTIONARY OF ART TERMS AND TECHNIQUES. New
York: Thomas Y. Crowell Co., (c. 1969). 447 pp. Color and black and
white illus., diagrams, photos. Bibliography.

> Reorganization of much of the material from MAYER'S ARTIST'S
> HANDBOOK, 1940, with the addition of current technical
> techniques and vocabulary. An effort has been made to stan-
> dardize nomenclature according to specific organization stan-
> dards. Helpful to the colorist in grasping concept of terminology.

*Pope, Arthur. THE LANGUAGE OF DRAWING & PAINTING. New York:
Russell & Russell, (c. 1929, 1931, 1949, 1968). ix, 162 pp. Black and white
illus., diagrams.

> A method for approaching the principles underlying representation
> in drawing and painting so that things executed in a variety of
> ways may be understood - particularly through the use of termi-
> nology proposed by the Colorimetry Committee of the Optical
> Society of America. Excellent source for distinction of differences
> between value and intensity, as well as brilliance and purity.

INDEX

Index

Index

Index

Index

Index

Index

Index

Index

Index

Index

Index

Index

Index

Index

Index

Index